Lecture Notes in Information Systems and Organisation

Volume 12

More information about this series at http://www.springer.com/series/11237

Felix Piazolo · Michael Felderer
Editors

Multidimensional Views on Enterprise Information Systems

Proceedings of ERP Future 2014

 Springer

Editors
Felix Piazolo
University of Innsbruck
Innsbruck
Austria

Michael Felderer
Institute of Computer Science
University of Innsbruck
Innsbruck
Austria

ISSN 2195-4968   ISSN 2195-4976   (electronic)
Lecture Notes in Information Systems and Organisation
ISBN 978-3-319-27041-8   ISBN 978-3-319-27043-2   (eBook)
DOI 10.1007/978-3-319-27043-2

Library of Congress Control Number: 2015955908

Printed on acid-free paper

This Springer imprint is published by SpringerNature
The registered company is Springer International Publishing AG Switzerland

Program Committee

Contents

Contributors

Dagmar Auer Institute for Application Oriented Knowledge Processing (FAW), Johannes Kepler University Linz (JKU), Linz, Austria

Peter Bollen Department of Organization and Strategy, School of Business Economics, Maastricht University, Maastricht, The Netherlands

Lars Brehm Munich University of Applied Sciences, Munich, Germany

Michal Dolezel University of Economics Prague, Prague, Czech Republic

Michael Felderer University of Innsbruck, Innsbruck, Austria

Eva-Maria Furtner IVM Institut für Verwaltungsmanagement GmbH, Innsbruck, Austria

Johannes Keckeis Department of Strategic Management, Marketing and Tourism, University of Innsbruck, Innsbruck, Austria

Bjoern Kemmoona Business Information Systems, University of Paderborn, Paderborn, Germany

Frederik Kramer Magdeburg Research and Competence Cluster (MRCC), Otto-von-Guericke-University, Magdeburg, Germany

Georg Krenn FH JOANNEUM, Industrial Management, Kapfenberg, Austria

Karl Kurbel Chair of Business Informatics, European University Viadrina Frankfurt (Oder), Frankfurt (Oder), Germany

Josef Küng Institute for Application Oriented Knowledge Processing (FAW), Johannes Kepler University Linz (JKU), Linz, Austria

Christian Leyh Technische Universität Dresden, Dresden, Germany

Robert Mertens Department of Computer Science, University of Applied Sciences Weserbergland, Hameln, Germany

Sven Mielke Department of Computer Science, University of Applied Sciences Weserbergland, Hameln, Germany

Stefan Nadschläger Institute for Application Oriented Knowledge Processing (FAW), Johannes Kepler University Linz (JKU), Linz, Austria

Dawid Nowak European University Viadrina Frankfurt (Oder), Frankfurt (Oder), Germany

Norbert Obermayr Dr. Obermayr GmbH, Linz, Austria

Wolfgang Ortner FH JOANNEUM, Industrial Management, Kapfenberg, Austria

Lukas Paa Andrássy University Budapest, Budapest, Hungary; Department of Strategic Management, Marketing and Tourism, University of Innsbruck, Innsbruck, Austria

Felix Piazolo University of Innsbruck, Innsbruck, Austria; Andrássy University Budapest, Budapest, Hungary

Sebastian Pospiech Cologne Intelligence GmbH, Decision Design, Cologne, Germany

Kurt Promberger Department of Strategic Management, Marketing and Tourism, University of Innsbruck, Innsbruck, Austria

Thomas Rehn InitOS GmbH & Co. KG, Magdeburg, Germany

Norbert Schlager-Weidinger IVM Institut für Verwaltungsmanagement GmbH, Innsbruck, Austria

Rainer Schmidt Munich University of Applied Sciences, Munich, Germany

Markus Schneider initOS GmbH & Co. KG, Magdeburg, Germany

Michael Städler Department of Computer Science, University of Applied Sciences Weserbergland, Hameln, Germany

Patrick Söhlke Next Vision GmbH, Hessisch Oldendorf, Germany

Klaus Turowski Magdeburg Research and Competence Cluster (MRCC), Otto-von-Guericke-University, Magdeburg, Germany

Harald Wildhölzl IVM Institut für Verwaltungsmanagement GmbH, Innsbruck, Austria

ERP Future 2014

Felix Piazolo and Michael Felderer

Abstract This is the introduction of the ERP Future 2014 Research Conference proceedings. It provides a short motivation and an overview of the topics covered by the conference.

Keywords Enterprise systems · Enterprise resource planning · Business processes · Business management · Business intelligence · Enterprise information systems · Software engineering · Innovation of enterprise information systems

Lately it seems as buzzwords like Digital Business, Digital Transformation or Smart Factory (Industry 4.0) are pushing topics related to conventional enterprise information systems into the background. The opposite is the case since those strongly promoted trends define a wider spectrum of requirements and very complex challenges regarding the enterprise information architecture and the involved enterprise systems alongside the holistic value chain of an integrated business environment. To remain successful and especially to gain competitive advantage it is necessary for private and public owned businesses and organizations to periodically question the appropriateness of the information technology in use. As strategic key resources to ensure efficient and effective end-to-end business processes enterprise information systems need to keep up with more and more important requirements such as connectivity, interoperability, information integration, security, process control, processual and technological flexibility, scalability, mass data handling and usability.

Disruptive innovations caused by the digital transformation era will strongly affect enterprise information systems and might not just lead to innovations in this domain but might also result in downstream disruptive innovations. This will not just be on a technological and processual but also on a service level and will lead to potential business model innovations. Multidimensional views on enterprise

F. Piazolo (✉)
Andrássy University Budapest, 1088 Budapest, Hungary
e-mail: felix.piazolo@andrassyuni.hu; felix.piazolo@uibk.ac.at

F. Piazolo · M. Felderer
University of Innsbruck, 6020 Innsbruck, Austria
e-mail: michael.felderer@uibk.ac.at

© Springer International Publishing Switzerland 2016   1
F. Piazolo and M. Felderer (eds.), *Multidimensional Views on Enterprise Information Systems*, Lecture Notes in Information Systems and Organisation 12,
DOI 10.1007/978-3-319-27043-2_1

information systems are necessary. An outlook into the future of enterprise information systems includes taking into account affecting parameters and their bidirectional influences. At the same time it is essential to study and learn from the past as well as to evaluate the given situation business are confronted with in the field of enterprise information systems.

The ERP Future 2014 Research conference is a scientific platform for research and innovation on enterprise information systems in general and specifically on core topics like business process management, business intelligence and enterprise resource planning systems. The event also addresses businesses developing, implementing and intensively using enterprise information systems since they will benefit directly from the research results and represent respectively are providing the object of investigation. To master the future challenges of enterprise information systems comprehensively, the ERP Future Research conference, as since 2012 [1, 2], accepted contributions with a business as well as an IT focus to consider enterprise information systems from various viewpoints. This combination of business and IT aspects is a unique characteristic of the conference that resulted in several valuable contributions with high theoretical as well as practical impact. Revised versions of these conference contributions are collected in the present proceedings of the ERP Future 2014 Research conference entitled 'Multidimensional Views on Enterprise Information Systems'.

The critical success factors [3] and configuration methods [4] for ERP implementation projects are analyzed and evaluated by first two contributions. Specific adoptions of ERP systems within small and medium enterprises are presented in addition [5]. Furthermore, an essential challenge of planning accuracy in ERP solutions, the input data, is addressed by one contribution [6].

Looking at the potential benefits of social software as a permanent input to ensure adequate business process management in ERP systems is discussed [7]. An approach to handle heterogeneous and unstructured business data to improve business processes is also presented [8]. Another contribution goes beyond classical knowledge work domains by analyzing knowledge-intensive business processes in farming. This prepares the basis for the requirements definition concerning amongst other things the IT support [9].

As optimization challenges in planning activities happen to be relevant in enterprise information systems in general it is discussed if SAP HANA is useful for optimization [10]. Modeling constructs that allow to model 'event-perspective' business rule semantics in a declarative way [11] and a concept towards productive enterprise systems testing is presented [12].

As the usability of software is one of the major actual and future requirements one contribution measures ERP usability from a user's perspective comparing different ERP solutions in use [13].

Instead of using business intelligence (BI) solutions solely as reporting tools the essential task of BI is to provide and identify information on the reasons for the presented results in classical reports. In a case study the impact of SAP HANA on BI strategy formulation is presented [14].

Finally, a concept of contract based planning in the public sector is presented and it is shown how this potential governmental planning method can be supported by ERP systems [15].

We thank all authors for their valuable contributions and the program committee members for their reviews. We hope that the collection of papers in the proceedings is interesting for the individual reader and enriching for the scientific community as well as for the industrial and business application.

Special thanks go to Manfred Vogt of the Vorarlberg University of Applied Sciences and his colleagues for their commitment and cooperativeness to host the ERP Future 2014 Research conference, Kurt Promberger and Christoph Weiss for initializing the ERP Future conferences in 2009, ACM German Chapter for supporting the conference, SIS Consulting as the premium sponsor and last but not least Andreas Hagn as the project manager and all members of the ERP Future 2014 team who enabled us to carry out such a successful and valuable conference.

Thank you,

Felix Piazolo, Michael Felderer

References

1. Piazolo, F., Felderer, M.: ERP future 2012. In: Piazolo, F., Felderer, M. (eds.) Innovation and Future of Enterprise Information Systems. ERP Future 2012 Research Conference Proceedings. Lecture Notes in Information Systems and Organisation, vol. 2, pp. 1–5. Springer, Berlin, Heidelberg (2013)
2. Piazolo, F., Felderer, M.: ERP future 2013. In: Piazolo, F, Felderer, M. (eds.) Novel Methods and Technologies for Enterprise Information Systems. ERP Future 2013 Research Conference Proceedings. Lecture Notes in Information Systems and Organisation, vol. 8, pp. 1–6. Springer, Berlin, Heidelberg (2014)
3. Leyh, C.: Critical success factors for ERP projects in small and medium-sized enterprises—the perspective of selected ERP system vendors. In: Piazolo, F., Felderer, M. (eds.) Multidimensional Views on Enterprise Information Systems. ERP Future 2014 Research Conference Proceedings. Lecture Notes in Information Systems and Organisation. Springer, Berlin, Heidelberg (2015)
4. Ortner, W., Krenn, G.: Are new configuration methods 'the key' to shorter ERP implementations? In: Piazolo, F., Felderer, M. (eds.) Multidimensional Views on Enterprise Information Systems. ERP Future 2014 Research Conference Proceedings. Lecture Notes in Information Systems and Organisation. Springer, Berlin, Heidelberg (2015)
5. Kramer, F., et al.: ERP-adoption within SME—challenging the existing body of knowledge with a recent case. In: Piazolo, F., Felderer, M. (eds.) Multidimensional Views on Enterprise Information Systems. ERP Future 2014 Research Conference Proceedings. Lecture Notes in Information Systems and Organisation. Springer, Berlin, Heidelberg (2015)
6. Obermayr, N.: Challenge detailed planning in ERP. In: Piazolo, F., Felderer, M. (eds) Multidimensional Views on Enterprise Information Systems. ERP Future 2014 Research Conference Proceedings. Lecture Notes in Information Systems and Organisation. Springer, Berlin, Heidelberg (2015)
7. Brehm, L., Schmidt, R.: Potential benefits of social business process management in the ERP domain. In: Piazolo, F., Felderer, M. (eds.) Multidimensional Views on Enterprise Information Systems. ERP Future 2014 Research Conference Proceedings. Lecture Notes in Information Systems and Organisation. Springer, Berlin, Heidelberg (2015)

8. Pospiech, S. et al.: Creating event logs from heterogeneous, unstructured business data. In: Piazolo, F., Felderer, M. (eds.) Multidimensional Views on Enterprise Information Systems. ERP Future 2014 Research Conference Proceedings. Lecture Notes in Information Systems and Organisation. Springer, Berlin, Heidelberg (2015)

9. Auer, D., Küng, J., Nadschläger, S.: Knowledge-intensive business processes—a case study for sustainable production in farms and forests. In: Piazolo F, Felderer M, (eds.) Multidimensional Views on Enterprise Information Systems. ERP Future 2014 Research Conference Proceedings. Lecture Notes in Information Systems and Organisation. Springer, Berlin, Heidelberg (2015)

10. Kurbel, K., Nowak, D.: Is SAP HANA useful for optimization?—An exploration of LP implementation alternatives. In: Piazolo, F., Felderer, M. (eds.) Multidimensional Views on Enterprise Information Systems. ERP Future 2014 Research Conference Proceedings. Lecture Notes in Information Systems and Organisation. Springer, Berlin, Heidelberg (2015)

11. Bollen, P.: Fact-based declarative business rule modeling for the static and dynamic perspectives in ERP applications. In: Piazolo, F., Felderer, M. (eds.) Multidimensional Views on Enterprise Information Systems. ERP Future 2014 Research Conference Proceedings. Lecture Notes in Information Systems and Organisation. Springer, Berlin, Heidelberg (2015)

12. Keckeis, J., Felderer, M.: Towards a concept for production enterprise ecosystem testing. In: Piazolo, F., Felderer, M. (eds.) Multidimensional Views on Enterprise Information Systems. ERP Future 2014 Research Conference Proceedings. Lecture Notes in Information Systems and Organisation. Springer, Berlin, Heidelberg (2015)

13. Paa, L., Piazolo, F.: Measuring ERP usability from the user's perspective. In: Piazolo, F., Felderer. M. (eds.) Multidimensional Views on Enterprise Information Systems. ERP Future 2014 Research Conference Proceedings. Lecture Notes in Information Systems and Organisation. Springer, Berlin, Heidelberg (2015)

14. Furtner, E., et al.: Impacts of SAP HANA on business intelligence (BI) strategy formulation. In: Piazolo, F., Felderer, M. (eds.) Multidimensional Views on Enterprise Information Systems. ERP Future 2014 Research Conference Proceedings. Lecture Notes in Information Systems and Organisation. Springer, Berlin, Heidelberg (2015)

15. Kemmoona, B.: Sequence of contracts as a means of planning in ERP-systems In: Piazolo, F., Felderer, M. (eds.) Multidimensional Views on Enterprise Information Systems. ERP Future 2014 Research Conference Proceedings. Lecture Notes in Information Systems and Organisation. Springer, Berlin, Heidelberg (2015)

Part I
Critical Success Factors of ERP Systems

Critical Success Factors for ERP Projects in Small and Medium-Sized Enterprises—The Perspective of Selected ERP System Vendors

Christian Leyh

Abstract The aim of our study was to provide a contribution to the research field of the critical success factors (CSFs) of ERP projects, with specific focus on smaller enterprises (SMEs). Therefore, we conducted a systematic literature review in order to update the existing reviews of CSFs. On the basis of that review, we led several interviews with ERP consultants experienced with ERP implementations in SMEs. As a result, we showed that all factors found in the literature also affected the success of ERP projects in SMEs. However, within those projects, technological factors gained much more importance compared to the factors that most influence the success of larger ERP projects. For SMEs, factors like the Organizational fit of the ERP system as well as ERP system tests were even more important than Top management support or Project management, which were the most important factors for large-scale companies.

Keywords ERP systems · Critical success factors · CSF · SME

1 Introduction

Today's enterprises are faced with the globalization of markets and fast changes in the economy. In order to cope with these conditions, the use of technology, as well as information and communication systems is almost mandatory. Specifically, the adoption of enterprise resource planning (ERP) systems as standardized systems that encompass the activities of entire enterprises has become an important factor for today's businesses. The demand for ERP applications has increased for several reasons, including competitive pressure to become low-cost producers, expectations of revenue growth, and the desire to re-engineer businesses to respond to market

C. Leyh (✉)
Chair of Information Systems, Esp. IS in Manufacturing and Commerce,
Technische Universität Dresden, 01062 Dresden, Germany
e-mail: christian.leyh@tu-dresden.de

© Springer International Publishing Switzerland 2016
F. Piazolo and M. Felderer (eds.), *Multidimensional Views on Enterprise Information Systems*, Lecture Notes in Information Systems and Organisation 12, DOI 10.1007/978-3-319-27043-2_2

challenges. A properly selected and implemented ERP system offers several benefits, such as considerable reductions in inventory costs, raw material costs, lead time for customers, production time, and production [1–4]. Therefore, the majority of enterprises around the world use ERP systems. For example, according to a survey conducted in Germany from 2010 to 2011, ERP systems are used in more than 92 % of all German industrial enterprises [5].

Due to the saturation of ERP markets targeting large-scale enterprises, ERP system manufacturers today are also now concentrating on the growing market of small and medium-sized enterprises (SMEs) [3, 6]. This has resulted in a highly fragmented ERP market and a great diffusion of ERP systems throughout enterprises of nearly every industry and every size [7–9]. Due to the strong demand and the high fragmentation of the market, there are many ERP systems with different technologies and philosophies available on the market. This multitude of software manufacturers, vendors, and systems implies that enterprises that use or want to use ERP systems must strive to find the "right" software as well as to be aware of the factors that influence the success of the implementation project.

The implementation of an information system (e.g., an ERP system) is a complex and time-consuming project during which companies face great opportunities, but at the same time also face enormous risks. To take advantage of the potential opportunities rather than get caught by the risks of these implementation projects, it is essential to focus on those factors that support a successful implementation of an information system [10, 11]. Being aware of these factors, a company can positively influence the success of the implementation project and effectively minimize the project's risks [10]. Recalling these so-called critical success factors (CSFs) is of high importance whenever a new system is to be adopted and implemented, or a running system needs to be upgraded or replaced. Errors during the selection, implementation, or maintenance of ERP systems, wrong implementation approaches, and ERP systems that do not fit the requirements of the enterprise can all cause financial disadvantages or disasters, perhaps even leading to insolvencies. Several examples of such negative scenarios can be found in the literature (e.g., [12, 13]). SMEs must be especially aware of the CSFs since they lack the financial, material, and personnel resources of larger companies. Thus, they are under greater pressure to implement and run ERP systems without failure and as smoothly as possible.

These critical success factors have already been considered in numerous scientific publications. Several case studies, surveys, and literature reviews have already been conducted by different researchers (e.g., [4, 14–16]). However, the existing ERP system success factor research has focused mostly on the selection and implementation of ERP systems in large enterprises. Less attention has been paid to the implementation projects in SMEs, despite the fact that research focusing on CSFs in smaller companies has been recommended in the research community for several years (e.g., [17, 18]).

Therefore, the aim of our study was to focus on the implementation of ERP systems in SMEs, especially focusing on the differences in CSFs of larger ERP projects and smaller projects. Prior to this study, we conducted a systematic literature review in order to update the existing reviews of CSFs. On the basis of the

CSFs identified, we conducted multiple interviews with German ERP consultants with specific experience in smaller ERP projects to obtain insights into the similarities and differences in CSFs for ERP system implementations in SMEs. Overall, our study was driven by the following research question:

Q1: What similarities and differences exist between critical success factors for ERP implementation projects in larger and smaller enterprises?

Therefore, the paper is structured as follows. The next section gives a short overview of the later discussed and important CSFs before the following section deals with the results of our literature review. There, we will point out which factors are the most important and which factors seem to have little influence on the success of an ERP implementation project. Next, our data collection methodology is described before the results of the interviews are presented and the research question is answered. Finally, the paper concludes with a summary of the results and discusses the limitations of our study.

2 Critical Success Factors Identified

A CSF for ERP projects has been defined by [15] as a reference to any condition or element that was deemed necessary in order for the ERP implementation to be successful. To provide a comprehensive understanding of the different CSFs and their concepts, they are described in this section before presenting the research methodology and discussing the results. However, only the most important and later-on discussed factors are described subsequently. The detailed definitions of the other CSFs can be found in [7, 19].

Balanced project team: In general, a project team consists of at least two persons working together for a common goal whereby each team member has defined responsibilities and functions [20]. The characteristics of the team members should complement each other, on their experience, their knowledge as well as their soft skills [21]. For an ERP implementation it is important to have a solid, core implementation team that is comprised of the organization's best and brightest individuals [15]. These team members should be assigned to the project on a fulltime basis. Only then they can fully concentrate on the project and are not disturbed or distracted with their daily business [22].

Change management: Change management involves early participation of all persons affected by a change process in order to reduce resistance against these changes. An important component is adequate training especially of the IT-department as well as an early communication of the changes to provide employees with an opportunity to react [23]. Change management strategies are responsible for handling the enterprise-wide cultural and structural changes. Therefore, it is necessary to train and educate the employees in various ways. Thereby, change management not only aims towards preventing rejection and supporting acceptance. Moreover, its goal is making employees understand and want the changes. Integrating the employees early in the planning and implementation process is important to achieve this understanding. Also, during the user training sessions a support team should be available in order to clarify and answer questions regarding the new processes and function. Furthermore, an additional evaluation with the end users should be accomplished after the "go live" to uncover problems and to avoid discords [24].

ERP system configuration: Since the initial ERP system version is based on best practices, a configuration or adaption of the system according to business processes is necessary in every ERP implementation project. Hence, as far as possible, the company should try to adopt the processes and options built into the ERP, rather than seek to modify the ERP [25]. Following [26], the more strongly the original ERP software is modified (e.g., even beyond the "normal" configuration) the smaller the chance is for a successful implementation project. Hence, a good business vision is helpful because it reduces the effort of capturing the functionality of the ERP business model and therefore minimizes the effort needed for the configuration [25]. Again, extensive system modifications will not only cause implementation problems, but also harm system maintenance. Therefore, fewer adjustments reduce the effort of integrating new versions, releases or updates [24].

ERP system tests: In ERP implementation, "go live" on the system without adequate and planned system testing may lead to an organizational disaster. Tests and validation of an ERP system is necessary to ensure that the system works technically correct and that the business process configurations were done in the right way [27]. Therefore testing and simulation exercises for both, the whole system and separate parts/functions, have to be performed during and in the final stages of the implementation process [15, 28].

Organizational fit of the ERP system: The fact that the organizational fit of an ERP system should be examined and considered comprehensively before its implementation sounds logical. Nevertheless, ERP manufacturers often try to create blind confidence in their ERP package even if the organizational fit is obviously low. In [26] is empirically examined the extent to which the implementation success of an ERP system depends on the fit between the company and the ERP system and found that the adaptation and configuration effort negatively correlates with the implementation success. Therefore, the careful selection of an ERP system with consideration of its company specific organizational fit, such as company size or industry sector, is essential. Thus, appropriate ERP system selection is an important factor in the effort to ensure a good fit between the company and the ERP system.

Project management: Project management refers to the ongoing management of the implementation plan [15]. The implementation of an ERP system is a unique procedure that requires enterprise-wide project management. Therefore, it involves the planning stages, the allocation of responsibilities, the definition of milestones and critical paths, training and human resource planning, and the determination of measures of success [23, 29]. This enables fast decisions and guarantees that such decisions are made by the "right" company members. Furthermore, continuous project management allows focus to remain on the important aspects of the ERP implementation and ensures that timelines and schedules are met [23]. Within project management, comprehensive documentation of the tasks, responsibilities, and goals is indispensable for the success of an ERP implementation [17].

Top management support and involvement: Top management support and involvement is one of the most important success factors for an ERP implementation [14]. Committed leadership at the top management level is the basis for the continuous accomplishment of every project [15]. Thus, innovations, in particular new technologies, are more quickly accepted by employees if these innovations are promoted by top management. Before the project starts, top management has to identify the peculiarities and challenges of the planned ERP implementation. Since many decisions that have to be made during the project can affect the whole enterprise, these decisions will need the acceptance and the commitment of the senior managers and often can only be made by them [30]. The commitment of top management is important in order for the allocation of necessary resources, quick and effective decision making, solutions of conflicts that need enterprise-wide acceptance, and supporting cooperation from all different departments [28].

User training: Missing or inadequate end user training is often a reason for failures in the implementation of new software. The main goal of end user training is to provide an effective understanding of the new business processes and applications as well as the new workflows that are created by the ERP implementation. Therefore, establishing a suitable plan for the employees' training is important [28]. Furthermore, during such an extensive project, management must determine which employee is the best fit for which position or for which application of the new software. This strongly depends on the employee's already acquired knowledge and/or additional training courses [31].

3 Literature Review of Critical Success Factors

In order to identify these factors that affect the success or failure of ERP projects, several case studies, surveys, and literature reviews have already been conducted by a number of researchers (e.g., [4, 15, 16, 24–26]).

However, most of the literature reviews cannot be reproduced, because descriptions of the review methods and procedures are lacking. Some researchers have pointed out the limitations of literature review articles, specifically noting that they lack methodological rigor [32]. Therefore, in order to update the existing reviews by including current ERP literature, we conducted a literature review by systematically reviewing articles in five different databases as well as papers drawn from several international conference proceedings. More specifically, we conducted two separate literature reviews according to the same search procedures and steps. The first was performed in mid-2010 [7, 19]. Since we identified 20 or more papers published each year, it was essential for us to update this review every 2 or 3 years. Therefore, we conducted the second review in mid-2013. The overall procedure for the literature review will not be part of this paper. It is described in detail in [7, 19, 33].

Table 1 Paper distribution

Year	Papers	Year	Papers
2013	30	2005	15
2012	31	2004	20
2011	39	2003	11
2010	37	2002	11
2009	42	2001	5
2008	22	2000	5
2007	24	1999	3
2006	24	1998	1

We identified 320 papers that referred to CSFs of ERP projects. These papers were reviewed again in depth in order to determine the various concepts associated with CSFs. For each paper, the CSFs were captured along with the publication year, the type of data collection used, and the companies (i.e., the number and size) from which the CSFs were derived. All 320 papers were published between 1998 and mid-2013. Table 1 shows the distribution of the papers by publication year. As is shown, most of the papers were published between 2006 and 2013.

Since 2004, each year around 20 papers and since 2009 each year around 30 papers or more papers about CSFs have been published. Therefore, it can be argued that a review every 2 or 3 years is reasonable in order to update the results of previously performed literature reviews, especially when considering the rapidly evolving technology and the changing system availability like the "Software-as-a-Service"-concept or ERP systems provided in the cloud.

Overall, 31 factors influencing the success of ERP system implementation were identified. Figure 1 shows the results of our review, i.e., the CSFs identified, their ranks and each factor's total number of occurrences in the reviewed papers. *Top management support and involvement, Project management*, and *User training* are the three most-named factors, with each being mentioned in more than 160 articles. Therefore, the factor *Top management support and involvement* is the outstanding rank #1 referred to in more than 200 papers. As mentioned above, we will not describe each factor and its concepts in detail in this paper. However, to provide a full understanding of the different CSFs and their concepts, we describe all 31 factors in [19] as well as the top eight factors again in more detail in [7].

Regarding the form of data collection, it must be stated that the papers consist of 144 single or multiple case studies, 118 surveys and 58 literature reviews or articles where CSFs are derived from the chosen literature.

In most previous literature reviews, the CSFs were grouped without as much attention to detail; therefore, a lower number of CSFs was used (e.g., [4, 15]). However, we took a different approach in our review. For the 31 factors, we used a larger number of categories than other researchers, as we expected the resulting distribution to offer more insight. If broader definitions for some CSFs might be needed at a later time, further aggregation of the categories is still possible. Comparing these results with other literature reviews (e.g., [15]), the top five factors are obviously similar, with only the ranked positions differing. Due to our large

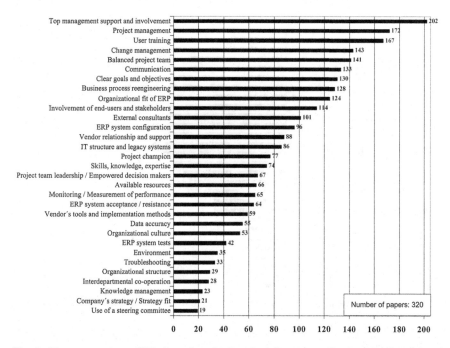

Fig. 1 Literature review—CSFs in rank order based on frequency of appearance in analyzed literature

literature base, the total numbers of observed mentions are much higher. Therefore, the differences in the CSF frequencies are much higher as well, making the distinctions in the significance of the factors clearer.

Concerning the company size during review 1 (conducted in mid-2010), only 12 papers explicitly focus on small and medium-sized enterprises (SMEs), mostly within single or multiple case studies. Within the review update (conducted in mid-2013), 25 articles dealt with SMEs explicitly. In some surveys, SMEs are included and analyzed as well, but they are a minority in these surveys. Therefore, deriving CSFs which are important for SMEs is difficult and can be seen as still lacking in the CSF research.

Within these 37 papers focusing on SMEs, *Top management support and involvement* (mentioned in 25 articles), *Project management* (mentioned in 25 articles) as well as *User training* (mentioned in 22 articles) are again the most frequently named factors for ERP projects in smaller enterprises (see Fig. 2).

However, the differences in the CSF frequencies are only minimal and may be related to the small number of identified papers. Therefore, deriving CSFs that are important for SMEs is difficult due to the small number of studies focusing solely on them. This clearly is a research gap in the ERP CSF research area. Therefore, our study focuses on this gap. We investigated these CSFs by interviewing German ERP consultants with specific experience in smaller ERP projects. The results will be part of the next sections.

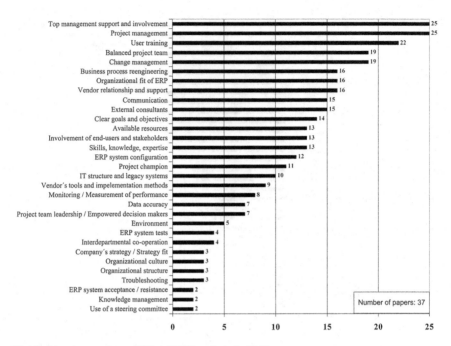

Fig. 2 Literature review—CSFs of ERP projects in SMEs

4 Critical Success Factors for SMEs' ERP Projects

4.1 Study Design—Data Collection Methodology

To gain an understanding of the differences in the CSFs for ERP system projects in large-scale enterprises and SMEs, we used a qualitative exploratory approach within German ERP system vendors.

The units of analysis in our study are the ERP projects for SMEs that the ERP consultants have performed so far in their career. For the data collection, we conducted several interviews with ERP consultants from German ERP system vendors to identify the factors that they determined to be relevant for the projects' success.

Therefore, we interviewed ten ERP consultants from six ERP system vendors. Table 5 in the Appendix gives an overview of the interviewed ERP consultants. Among the ERP consultants, we were able to interview some consultants with longtime experience in more than 100 ERP projects as well as some consultants who had been working in this field for only a few years and had experience with fewer than 10 ERP projects (see Table 5).

To gain a deep and detailed view of the consultants' experiences, we chose direct structured interviews as our method of data collection. The interviews were conducted in retrospect to the ERP projects between April and July 2013. The interviews were designed as partially standardized interviews using open to semi-open questions as initial starting points for the conversation. Both personal (face-to-face) interviews, as well as telephone interviews, were conducted by the author. An interview guideline was developed, based on the questions of [34], who conducted a similar study, as well as on the basis of one of our previous CSF studies that had another focus [35]. We changed the questions to align with our identified CSFs (see Fig. 1) to ensure that all of the factors were discussed in the interviews. The interview guideline consisted of 52 main questions with further sub-questions which referred to the 31 identified CSFs. These questions were formulated in an open way so that it would be possible to identify "new" CSFs which were not resulting from the literature review. This questionnaire was sent to interviewees before the interviews took place to allow them to prepare for their interviews.

For a better analysis of the results, we recorded all interviews (the interviews typically took between 70 and 180 min) and transcribed them afterwards (resulting in about 250 pages of written text). As a first step, non-verbal and para-linguistic elements and other elements that were not relevant to the study were excluded. Afterwards, to evaluate the CSFs, the interviews were analyzed with reference to each CSF question block. We matched the answers and statements of the interviewees to the respective factor. Then, each CSF was ranked according to a three-tier scale (2-very important factor; 1-important factor; 0-less/non-important factor), and, for a finer classification, according to a five-tier scale (4-very important factor; 3-important factor; 2-factor was seen as relevant; 1-factor was mentioned but not seen as being very relevant; 0-factor was not seen as relevant or important/factor was not mentioned at all). This rating was done regarding the respective statements of the interviewees. We used these two scales to gain a preliminary understanding of whether differences would occur by using a finer/more detailed scale. Here, the five-tier-scale could be seen as more appropriate for determining the importance of the factors. After setting up this ranking of CSFs, we discussed the factor rating with other researchers in this field to reduce the subjectivity of the rating. Finally, this procedure resulted in a ranking of all 31 CSFs according to the interviewees' statements and answers.

4.2   Results of the Interviews

For each interview, a ranking of the critical success factors was set up by the author. A final ranking was created including all interviews and all individual rankings (see Table 2). As shown, the most important factors for ERP implementation projects in small and medium-sized companies according to our study are *ERP system tests* and *Organizational fit of the ERP system* with more than 30 out of a possible 40 points. Also, no further factors could be identified during the interviews. Each of the 31 factors stemming from the literature review was mentioned by at least one interviewee. However, the factors *Organizational structure*, *Troubleshooting* and *Interdepartmental cooperation* were in fact mentioned by some interviewees but these factors were not seen as really important. They were rated with less than five out of 40 possible points.

Table 2 CSFs according the five-tier-scale rating

Rank	Factor	Factor rating	Rank	Factor	Factor rating
1	Organizational fit of the ERP system	31	17	External consultants	18
	ERP system tests	31		Involvement of end-users and stakeholders	18
3	Balanced project team	28		Data accuracy	18
	Project management	28	20	Organizational culture	17
5	Change management	27	21	Vendor relationship and support	15
6	Clear goals and objectives	26		Vendor's tools and implementation methods	15
	Communication	26	23	Project champion	13
8	Top management support and involvement	25		Environment	13
	User training	25		Knowledge management	13
10	ERP system configuration	24		Skills, knowledge, and expertise	13
11	Use of a steering committee	23	27	IT structure and legacy systems	11
12	Company's strategy/strategy fit	22	28	Business process reengineering	10
13	Monitoring and performance measurement	20	29	Troubleshooting	4
14	Available resources	19	30	Organizational structure	1
	Project team leadership/empowered decision makers	19	31	Interdepartmental cooperation	0
	ERP system acceptance/resistance	19			

4-very important factor; 3-important factor; 2-factor was seen as relevant; 1-factor was mentioned but not seen as being very relevant; 0-factor was not seen as relevant or important/factor was not mentioned at all) / maximum possible rating on basis of 10 interviews = 40

Neither of the two most important factors were part of the top 5 within the ranking of the literature review (see Table 3). The factor *ERP system tests* was not even part of the top 20 within the literature review (see Figs. 1 and 2). Also, *Organizational fit of the ERP system* has gained more importance, according to our interviewees. The importance of both factors indicates that SMEs are forced to find the right ERP system that fits their needs and to test the system properly before the Go-Live. As mentioned in the first section, due to their lack of the financial, material, and personnel resources compared to larger companies', failures during or

Table 3 Comparison of the top five factors

Rank	Results of the literature review (all company sizes)	Results of the literature review (only SMEs)	Factors from the interviews
1	Top management support and involvement	Top management support and involvement	Organizational fit of the ERP system
			ERP system tests
2	Project management	Project management	
3	User training	User training	Balanced project team
			Project management
4	Change management	Balanced project team	
		Change management	
5	Balanced project team		Change management

after the Go-Live can easily cause financial disadvantages or disasters, perhaps even leading to the insolvency of such small companies. Therefore, this is supported by the importance of the top two factors in our study.

Reasons for this can also be seen in the highly fragmented ERP system market as well as in the increasing multitude of software manufacturers and ERP systems. Enterprises are facing more and more difficulties in identifying the best fitting ERP system. Therefore, more emphasis is laid on the selection of the "right" ERP system with a high *Organizational fit of the ERP system*. This also supports the statement that SMEs strongly depend on ERP systems that fit their needs even more than large companies may. SMEs cannot afford to be restricted by stiff ERP processes; moreover, it is important that the system is adapted according to their own processes. This can also be seen by looking at *Business process reengineering*. This factor was part of the top 10 in the literature review (see Figs. 1 and 2) but is ranked at #28 in our study with only 10 out of 40 possible points (see Table 2). Here, SMEs seek more to adapt the system than to change the business processes.

To categorize critical success factors, in [25] a matrix scheme is suggested. Here, the authors consider the tactical or strategic direction of the CSFs and divide them into organizational and technological factors. Thus, tactical CSFs rather relate to short-term aspects and goals of the system implementation project itself, whereby strategic factors aim towards long-term impacts of activities with strong connections to the development of the organization in relation to mission, vision and core competencies of the business activity. Considering the technological and organizational character of the CSFs, the specificity and significance of technological factors are strongly dependent on the ERP systems themselves, whereas organizational factors focus on corporate culture and its environment with its specific processes and structures [25, 36, 37]. Table 4 gives an overview of the categorization of the identified CSFs in our study with a focus on their ranking.

We oriented the classification and categorization of the factors according to [36, 37]. The factors of the top 10 are highlighted. It is shown that only a few CSFs (six out of 31) are technological factors whereas more than 50 % of the factors (17 out

Table 4 Categorization of CSFs (Model adapted from [25, 36, 37])

	Strategic		Tactical	
Organizational	**Critical Success Factors**	**Rank**	**Critical Success Factors**	**Rank**
	Balanced project team	**3**	**Project management**	**3**
	Change management	**5**	**Communication**	**6**
	Clear goals and objectives	**6**	**User training**	**8**
	Top management support and involvement	**8**	Monitoring/measurement of performance	13
	Use of a steering committee	11	External consultants	17
	Company's strategy/strategy fit	12	Skills, knowledge and expertise	23
	Available resources	14	Troubleshooting	29
	Project team leadership/empowered decision makers	14	Interdepartmental cooperation	31
	ERP system acceptance/resistance	14		
	Involvement of end-users and stakeholders	17		
	Organizational culture	20		
	Vendor relationship and support	21		
	Project champion	23		
	Environment	23		
	Knowledge management	23		
	Business process reengineering	28		
	Organizational structure	30		
Technological	**Organizational fit of the ERP system**	**1**	**ERP system tests**	**1**
	ERP system configuration	**10**	Data accuracy	17
			Vendor's tools and implementation methods	21
			IT structure and legacy systems	27

of 31) are organizational factors with a strategic characteristic. Though the top 10 factors are spread out among all four categories, most of them are part of the organizational category. Remarkably, the two most important factors are part of the technological view. This supports the statement above that the technological aspects of ERP projects and their impact on the enterprises are considered more important for SMEs than for larger companies. However, smaller enterprises and ERP vendors should consider both the organizational and technological aspects when implementing an ERP system.

5 Conclusion and Limitations

The aim of our study was to gain insight into the research field of CSFs for ERP implementation projects, with a focus on ERP projects in small and medium-sized enterprises. Research in the field of ERP system projects and their CSFs provides valuable information that may enhance the degree to which an organization's implementation project succeeds [15]. As a first step, we carried out a systematic literature review to identify CSFs and to update existing reviews. Our review turned up a variety of papers, i.e., case studies, surveys, and literature reviews, focusing on CSFs. All in all, we identified 320 relevant papers dealing with CSFs of ERP system projects. From these existing studies, we derived 31 different CSFs (see Fig. 1). Most of the identified papers and studies focus on large companies. Small and medium-sized enterprises are—if included at all—usually underrepresented in quantitative studies. Studies exclusively focusing on SMEs are rare. We identified 37 of the 320 articles with this explicit focus. These are only nearly 12 % of all published papers with a focus on CSF. Even if research focusing on CSFs in smaller companies has been recommended in the research community for several years (e.g., [17, 18]), our reviews reveal that SMEs are still not the primary focus of CSF research. Therefore, this can still be seen as a clear lack of research.

To this end, we set up a study with a specific SME focus. We conducted several interviews with ERP consultants experienced with ERP implementations in SMEs. Using a guideline consisting of 52 initial questions about CSFs, we conducted ten interviews. We found that all 31 factors found in the literature review were mentioned by at least one interviewee, and therefore all 31 factors also somehow affect the success of the ERP system projects in SMEs, except the factor *Interdepartmental cooperation* that was mentioned by some interviewees but not seen as relevant for ERP projects in SMEs. However, contrary to the ranking resulting from the literature review, we identified factors with a more technological focus being important for those ERP projects. Here, the factors *ERP system tests* and *Organizational fit of the ERP system* as the most important factors as well as *ERP system configuration* that is also part of the top 10 factors refer to more technological aspects. Hence, factors with an organizational characteristic could also be identified as part of the top 5 factors in our study (*Balanced project team*, *Project management*, and *Change management*).

Regarding the research question, our study could show that most of the factors which influence the success of ERP system implementation projects in large-scale enterprises also have influence on ERP projects in SMEs. We could not identify any further factors that were not already referred to in the literature. However, we could show that the importance of the factors differs a lot and that SMEs and also the ERP manufacturers have to be aware of these differences in the factors' characteristics, focusing also on technological aspects of the ERP implementations rather than focusing mainly on the organizational factors, as they are more important for the large-scale companies.

A few limitations of our study must be mentioned as well. For our literature review, we are aware that we cannot be certain that we have identified all relevant papers published in journals and conferences since we made a specific selection of five databases and five international conferences. Therefore, journals not included in our databases and the proceedings from other conferences might also provide relevant articles. Another limitation is the coding of the CSFs. We tried to reduce any subjectivity by formulating coding rules and by discussing the coding of the CSFs with several independent researchers. However, other researchers may code the CSFs in other ways. For the interview study, the interviews conducted and data evaluated represent only an investigation of sample ERP projects in SMEs based on the experiences of the ERP consultants. These results are limited to the specifics of these projects. In light of this, we will conduct further case studies and some larger surveys to broaden the results of this investigation.

Appendix

Table 5 Overview of the ERP consultants and their experience

ERP manufacturer	ERP consultant	ERP consultant since	Experience with ERP projects
Manufacturer 1	Consultant 1	Active in the ERP business for more than 30 years	Carried out more than 100 ERP projects
Manufacturer 2	Consultant 2	User support and project support for three years	Carried out three ERP projects
Manufacturer 3	Consultant 3	ERP consultant since 2008	Carried out eight ERP projects
	Consultant 4	ERP consultant and Head of project management for Manufacturer 3 since 2013	More than 30 years of experience with ERP topics and ERP projects as employee of several SMEs
Manufacturer 4	Consultant 5	ERP consultant for Manufacturer 4 since 2011	More than 30 years of experience with ERP topics and ERP projects as employee of several SMEs and other ERP manufacturers
	Consultant 6	ERP consultant since 2000; by now Head of Branch Office for Manufacturer 4	Carried out seven ERP projects; by now as Head of Branch Office support for 50 parallel ERP projects
Manufacturer 5	Consultant 7	ERP consultant for more than 16 years	Carried out more than 100 ERP projects
	Consultant 8	ERP consultant for more than 13 years	Carried out around 130 ERP projects
Manufacturer 6	Consultant 9	ERP consultant for several years	Carried out several ERP projects (detailed number was not stated)
	Consultant 10	ERP consultant since 2010	Carried out five ERP projects

References

1. Davenport, T.H.: Mission Critical: Realizing the Promise of Enterprise Systems. Harvard Business School Press, Boston (2000)
2. Grabski, S.V., Leech, S.A.: Complementary controls and ERP implementation success. Int. J. Acc. Inf. Syst. **8**(1), 17–39 (2007)
3. Koh, S.C.L., Simpson, M.: Change and uncertainty in SME manufacturing environments using ERP. J. Manuf. Technol. Manag. **16**(6), 629–653 (2005)
4. Somers, T.M., Nelson, K.: The impact of critical success factors across the stages of enterprise resource planning implementations. In: Proceedings of the 34th Hawaii International Conference on System Sciences (HICSS 2001), 3–6 Jan 2001, Hawaii, USA (2001)
5. Konradin GmbH: Konradin ERP-Studie 2011—Einsatz von ERP-Lösungen in der Industrie. Konradin Mediengruppe, Leinfelden-Echterdingen, Germany (2011)
6. Deep, A., Guttridge, P., Dani, S., Burns, N.: Investigating factors affecting ERP selection in the made-to-order SME sector. J. Manuf. Technol. Manag. **19**(4), 430–446 (2008)
7. Leyh, C.: Critical success factors for ERP system implementation projects: a literature review. In: Møller, C., Chaudhry, S. (eds.): Advances in Enterprise Information Systems II, pp. 45–56. CRC Press/Balkema, Leiden, The Netherlands (2012)
8. Winkelmann, A., Klose, K.: Experiences while selecting, adapting and implementing ERP systems in SMEs: a case study. In: Proceedings of the 14th Americas Conference on Information Systems (AMCIS 2008), 14–17 Aug 2008, Paper 257. Toronto, Ontario, Canada (2008)
9. Winkelmann, A., Leyh, C.: Teaching ERP systems: a multi-perspective view on the ERP system market. J. Inf. Syst. Educ. **21**(2), 233–240 (2010)
10. Jones, A., Robinson, J., O'Toole, B., Webb, D.: Implementing a bespoke supply chain management system to deliver tangible benefits. Int. J. Adv. Manuf. Technol. **30**(9/10), 927–937 (2006)
11. Ngai, E.W.T., Cheng, T.C.E., Ho, S.S.M.: Critical success factors of web-based supply-chain management systems: an exploratory study. Prod. Plan. Control **15**(6), 622–630 (2004)
12. Barker, T., Frolick, M.N.: ERP Implementation Failure: a case study. Inf. Syst. Manag. **20**(4), 43–49 (2003)
13. Hsu, K., Sylvestre, J., Sayed, E.N.: Avoiding ERP pitfalls. J. Corp. Acc. Finan. **17**(4), 67–74 (2006)
14. Achanga, P., Nelde, G., Roy, R., Shehab, E.: Critical success factors for lean implementation within SMEs. J. Manuf. Technol. Manag. **17**(4), 460–471 (2006)
15. Finney, S., Corbett, M.: ERP implementation: a compilation and analysis of critical success factors. Bus. Process Manag. J. **13**(3), 329–347 (2007)
16. Nah, F.F.-H., Zuckweiler, K.M., Lau, J.L-S.: ERP implementation: chief information officers' perceptions of critical success factors. Int. J. Hum.-Comput. Interact. **16**(1), 5–22 (2003)
17. Snider, B., da Silveira, G.J.C., Balakrishnan, J.: ERP implementation at SMEs: analysis of five Canadian cases. Int. J. Oper. Prod. Manag. **29**(1), 4–29 (2009)
18. Sun, A.Y.T., Yazdani, A., Overend, J.D.: Achievement assessment for enterprise resource planning (ERP) system implementations based on critical success factors (CSFs). Int. J. Prod. Econ. **98**(2), 189–203 (2005)
19. Leyh, C.: Critical success factors for ERP system selection, implementation and post-implementation. In: Léger, P.-M., Pellerin, R., Babin, G. (eds.): Readings on Enterprise Resource Planning, Chap. 5, pp. 63–77. ERPsim Lab, HEC Montreal, Montreal (2011)
20. Humphrey, W.S.: Introduction to the Team Software Process. Addison-Wesley, Amsterdam (1999)
21. Hesseler, M., Goertz, M.: Basiswissen ERP-Systeme—Auswahl, Einführung & Einsatz betriebswirtschaftlicher Standardsoftware.W3 l, Witten, Germany (2007)

22. Shanks, G., Parr, A.: A model of ERP project implementation. J. Inf. Technol. **15**(4), 289–303 (2000)
23. Al-Mashari, M., Al-Mudimigh, A.: ERP Implementation: lessons from a case study. Inf. Technol. People **16**(1), 21–33 (2003)
24. Loh, T.C., Koh, S.C.L.: Critical elements for a successful enterprise resource planning implementation in small-and medium-sized enterprises. Int. J. Prod. Res. **42**(17), 3433–3455 (2004)
25. Esteves-Sousa, J., Pastor-Collado, J.: Towards the unification of critical success factors for ERP implementations. In: Proceedings of the 10th Annual Business Information Technology Conference (BIT 2000). Manchester, UK (2000)
26. Hong, K.-K., Kim, Y.-G.: The critical success factors for ERP implementation: an organizational fit perspective. Inf. Manag. **40**(1), 25–40 (2002)
27. Appelrath, H., Ritter, J.: SAP R/3 Implementation: Method and Tools. Springer, Berlin (2000)
28. Al-Mashari, M., Al-Mudimigh, A., Zairi, M.: enterprise resource planning: a taxonomy of critical factors. Eur. J. Oper. Res. **146**(2), 352–364 (2003)
29. Nah, F.F-H., Lau, J.L-S., Kuang, J.: Critical factors for successful implementation of enterprise systems. Bus. Process Manag. J. **7**(3), 285–296 (2001)
30. Becker, J., Vering, O., Winkelmann, A.: Softwareauswahl und–einführung in Industrie und Handel: Vorgehen bei und Erfahrungen mit ERP- und Warenwirtschaftssystemen. Springer, Berlin (2007)
31. Teich, I., Kolbenschlag, W., Reiners, W.: Der richtige Weg zur Softwareauswahl. Springer, Berlin (2008)
32. Vom Brocke, J., Simons, A., Niehaves, B., Riemer, K., Plattfaut, R., Cleven, A.: Reconstructing the giant: on the importance of rigour in documenting the literature search process. In: Proceedings of the 17th European Conference on Information Systems (ECIS 2009), 8–10 June 2009, Verona, Italy (2009)
33. Leyh, C.: Which factors influence ERP implementation projects in small and medium-sized enterprises? In: Proceedings of the 20th Americas Conference on Information Systems (AMCIS 2014), 7–9 Aug 2014, Savanah, Georgia, USA (2014)
34. Nah, F.F.-H., Delgado, S.: Critical success factors for enterprise resource planning implementation and upgrade. J. Comput. Inf. Syst. **46**(29), 99–113 (2006)
35. Leyh, C., Muschick, P.: Critical success factors for ERP system upgrades—The case of a German large-scale Enterprise. In: Proceedings of the 19th Americas Conference on Information Systems (AMCIS 2013), 15–17 Aug 2013, Chicago, Illinois, USA (2013)
36. Esteves-Sousa, J.: Definition and Analysis of Critical Success Factors for ERP Implementation Projects. Barcelona, Spain (2004)
37. Remus, U.: Critical success factors for implementing enterprise portals: a comparison with ERP implementations. Bus. Process Manag. J. **13**(4), 538–552 (2007)

Are New Configuration Methods 'the Key' to Shorter ERP Implementations?

Wolfgang Ortner and Georg Krenn

Abstract Are cloud-based business platforms faster to implement in small and medium-sized enterprises (SMEs)? The aim of this contribution is to evaluate new configuration methods and its effects on ERP projects. Therefore, experiences of several implementations of the cloud-based business platform SAP Business ByDesign in SMEs are collected and analyzed. This applied research paper shows concrete product-related configuration features and its effects on the real companies of the case studies conducted. The outcome is seen as recommendation for companies in comparable situations, but is not representative and not directly transferable to other products. Nevertheless, the question of (new) accelerators for ERP implementations is examined in general.

Keywords ERP implementation · Configuration · Implementation time

1 Introduction

In recent years also Enterprise Resource Planning systems (ERP systems) were fundamentally influenced by major trends in information technology (IT) and technological enhancements [1, 2]. Trends seen across many ERP systems cover mobility, cloud computing, integration, social collaboration and improved user interfaces [1]. Besides the well-known 'mega trends', new and innovative approaches were also made regarding the self-enablement of users, the provisioning of integrated 'end-to-end' process scenarios and integral and highly standardized implementation configuration methodologies [3]. Although end users normally will not see the configuration area of an ERP system, in this contribution, we focus on

W. Ortner (✉) · G. Krenn
FH JOANNEUM, Industrial Management, Werk-VI-Str. 46, Kapfenberg 8605, Austria
e-mail: wolfgang.ortner@fh-joanneum.at

G. Krenn
e-mail: georg.krenn@fh-joanneum.at

© Springer International Publishing Switzerland 2016   23
F. Piazolo and M. Felderer (eds.), *Multidimensional Views on Enterprise Information Systems*, Lecture Notes in Information Systems and Organisation 12, DOI 10.1007/978-3-319-27043-2_3

this specific product innovation, because we see this mechanism as a possible crucial element to reduce ERP implementation times—an issue that was known as 'top problem area' in the 1990s ERP research [4]. Therefore, this issue is regarded as highly relevant for small and medium-sized enterprises.

To answer the research question, whether the integral configuration method has positive effects on ERP implementation times, this product innovation is presented in the context of ERP implementation and its relevant factors of success. To get a better understanding of this new method, the differences to the traditional way of customizing are indicated. To gain experiences using that mechanism of configuration and also to learn about effects on the organization using the new standardized implementation method, we collected data out of case studies based on real ERP implementations. All cases are described according to the overall relevant factors of success of an ERP implementation [5].

1.1 Does a Modern Configuration Reduce the Implementation Time of ERP?

Within this contribution it is examined whether modern configuration methods of ERP systems really simplify the customization and, hence, reduce implementation times and configuration efforts in ERP implementation projects. Based on case studies of the implementation of the on demand solution SAP Business ByDesign in SMEs the configuration methodology is analyzed according to the following questions:

- How does the new integral configuration contribute to ERP implementation projects?
- Analyze and discuss the effects on ERP implementations especially for small and medium sized enterprises.

1.2 Methodology

In order to create a measurement scheme for analyzing the different case studies the integral method of business configuration, its specific approach and components are outlined first. The measurement scheme then is used to describe and evaluate the different implementations in real companies—general critical factors of success are derived. As result it is shown, that there is huge positive impact for implementations as well as for future change projects that finally could lead to improved flexibility in ERP use.

2 ERP Implementations in Small and Medium-Sized Enterprises

2.1 History of Customizing and Implementation

Analyzing the market and use of business information systems at the end of the first decade of the 21st century we have to state, that in bigger companies Enterprise Resource Planning systems have become a 'quasi standard'. Standard software packages, which integrate value and material flow based on real-time transactions cover a wide range of companies' functions and hierarchical levels [6–8].

Conceptually, these systems follow two major visions: the vision of having business administrative consistent data through integration of data, functions and methods [9] that were discussed for example in the "Kölner Integrationsmodell" [10] or in concepts like "Architecture of Integrated Information Systems" (ARIS; [11]). And, on the other hand, the vision of having one system for all types of company. Hypothesis of that idea is the independence of the structure of a business from its content. These business information systems provide highly configurable process scenarios that were stored in a process library or 'reference model' [12]. During the implementation of the software, the customizing has to ensure, that the company's requirements are met.

It was the process of customizing and the implementation projects themselves that lead to many problems and discussions. Because of the extensive options to configure these systems, the overall complexity became extremely high. It took years to become expert in a module and because of technical progress and changes of releases, experts could only master the parameterization of one or a few modules. Projects of ERP implementation tended to exceed time and budget and were critically discussed in literature (i.e. [13, 14]).

Reto v. Arb, who conducted a study analyzing software implementations of SAP R/3, found out that the complexity of the system, release changes and also the lack of know-how of external consultants were among the top problem issues, when implementing the ERP system [4]. Especially the technical issues could be positively influenced by the new method of configuring that has been released with on demand solutions like SAP's Business ByDesign: less complexity through the integrated business-oriented configuration, no more updating effort for the customer through the software as a service (SaaS) model. Breaking these classical problem areas could lead to shorter and easier implementations and could therefore be relevant for small and medium sized enterprises. In this context it has to be stated, that it was never the technical area alone that led to problems and/or discussions in ERP implementations. Other factors of success have been determined through different research activities and address also the management and organizational aspects of an ERP implementation. Gerhardter's literature research shows, these factors in an overview [15].

The factors of success of a classical ERP implementation show, that the organizational and managerial area still has to be addressed during an ERP implementation. Beside the technical improvements of the new configuration method, which is an integral part of the system, the whole process of implementation is supported with project management tools. In the next paragraph the business-oriented configuration method are introduced and discussed with reference to the findings of literature research.

2.2 Business-Oriented ERP Configuration

In contrast to traditional ERP configuration an integral business oriented configuration allows users to adjust and configure the system and its behavior without requiring any technical know-how [5].

In this contribution the 'business configuration' of SAP Business ByDesign is analyzed. The goal is to give a concrete example on how a business-oriented configuration works and supports the critical factors of success of an ERP implementation. The description given is based on the analysis of a reference system in combination with the explanations given by Hufgard/Krüger [3].

The process of configuration follows a step-by-step procedure, defined according to the implementation project management method SAP Launch, which is used universally across all SaaS implementations of SAP [21].

The methodology consist of four phases with partly overlapping tasks and milestones (see Fig. 4). The first phase ('prepare') includes tasks like the definition of goals, main concepts for the business processes, the scope to be implemented and the organizational structure to be reflected in the system. The phase model itself and the phase of defining goals and the organizational involvement of the management already address at least three factors of success mentioned in Table 1. Followed by the 'realize' phase focusing on the fine-tuning of the system, possible customer-specific developments, integration scenarios and the data migration are addressed. The main goal is to get an accepted configuration of the system. The configuration is tested in the 'verify' phase. The system is prepared for go-live and the cutover is thoroughly planned. At the end a go-live readiness is achieved and the cutover is executed in the 'launch' phase [3, 21].

While the milestones are tightly linked to the phases some of the tasks overlap phases (see Fig. 4). Especially the key user enablement is seen as a continuous tasks with different focus areas along the project. This addresses the success factor of user involvement in Table 1. The data migration stream starts in an earlier phase and eventually finishes during the verification phase of the system [3, 21].

With the phase model, which is visualized in Fig. 1, the business-oriented configuration described includes a project management method that combines the implementation project's tasks seamlessly with a time frame needed for a safe Go-Live procedure. The whole configuration process follows a logical sequence of tasks. This means, that earlier steps of configuration influence the dependent tasks

Table 1 Literature analysis: critical success factors of a classical ERP implementation

Criteria	Author					
	v. Arb, 1997 [4]	Blume, 1997 [16]	Brand, 1999 [17]	Umble/Haft/Umble, 2003 [18]	Esteves/Pastor, 2005 [19]	Siegenthaler/Schmid, 2005 [20]
Involvement and training of the users	✓	✓	✓	✓	✓	✓
Project management	✓	✓	✓	✓	✓	✓
Commitment of top management	✓	✓		✓	✓	✓
Clearly formulated project objectives	✓	✓	✓	✓	✓	
Method of the implementation approach	✓	✓	✓	✓	✓	
Technical requirements	✓	✓	✓	✓	✓	✓
Risk of consultancy	✓	✓			✓	✓
Reorganization of business processes	✓	✓		✓	✓	
Time and resource management	✓	✓			✓	✓
Contract drafting	✓				✓	

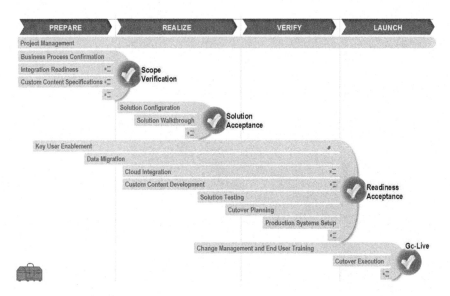

Fig. 1 Launch implementation methodology: phases, tasks and milestones (© SAP AG) [21]

and activities. This is a major difference to the classical customizing method, where the consistency of parameters had to be ensured mainly by the person entering the parameters.

The configuration is started by defining 'the scope of the implementation'. This 'scoping' is used to select countries, business areas and processes for the implementation which are then configured by answering 'yes' or 'no' questions to enable/disable specific elements of the system. These elements and their structure are part of the 'Business Adaption Catalog' (BAC) which contains the functional capabilities of the solution and ensures a continuous adaption to scope and behavior of the solution throughout its lifecycle.

Based on the selected scope and the answers to the business questions an 'activity list' is maintained containing tasks regarding the detailed system configuration ('fine-tuning'), 'data migration', 'integration' and 'extension aspects', 'project management' and 'go-live activities'. Changes in the scoping are directly reflected in the activity list by adding or removing tasks. The configuration comprises both parts into an 'implementation project' which defines the functional content of the system and its behavior along business processes. The implementation project (see Fig. 2) is used as a project management instrument reflecting scoping decisions, giving an overview of open and finished tasks in the activity list and showing the implementation status in a milestone overview.

The implementation project in Fig. 2 shows the selected country (Austria) and business areas such as marketing, sales, service and e.g. cash flow management. The areas include elements arranged in a hierarchical order. For example, the business area of sales includes the business topics 'account and activity management',

Project Overview: First Implementation

| Close | Edit Project Scope | Open Activity List | View Project History | Apply Implementation Project Template |

General Information

Title:	First Implementation
Description:	Initial Implement
Owner:	All administrators
Involved Areas:	Marketing, Sales, Service, Sourcing, Purchasing, Product Development, Supply Chain Planning and Control, Manufacturing, Warehousing, and Logistics, Supply Chain Setup Management, Project Management, Cash Flow Management, Financial and Management Accounting, Travel and Expenses, Human Resources, Business Performance Management, Communication and Information Exchange, Compliance, General Business Data, Built-in Services and Support

Countries

Austria

Types of Business

Scoping

Elements you selected:	53
Elements you deselected:	1
Questions you reviewed:	916
Questions you did not review:	74

Planned Implementation Timeline

Start Date:	15.01.2012
End Date:	15.03.2012
Status:	Started

Activities

Activities you added manually:	0
Activities added automatically:	158

List of Milestones

Title	Status	Confirmed On
Confirm Milestone: Design Accepted	✓	28.10.2010 14:21
Confirm Milestone: Solution Accepted	◇	
Confirm Milestone: Go-Live Readiness Acceptance	◇	28.10.2010 14:21

Fig. 2 Screenshot of an implementation project overview (© SAP AG)

'product and service portfolio', 'new businesses, 'selling products and services',' 'customer invoicing' and 'sales planning'. The topic 'new business' is further divided into the options 'lead management', 'opportunities', 'sales quotes', 'communication for new business' and 'analysis for new business' which contain relevant questions. Each business area, topic, option and question in the BAC has a general description, states its relevance and shows its dependency to other elements. The selection of one element might therefore result in automatic selection of dependent elements by the system. This ensures an always consistent business configuration. If consistency rules require a specific element it is added with a standardized configuration and does not require the user to check the configuration. The scoping influences the activity list, the views within configuration elements of the activity list, backend configurations, access to functional areas in the system and the process control.

The organizational structure of the implementing enterprise is configured in the system via an organizational chart which reflects the hierarchical structure of companies, residences, profit and cost centers and functional responsibilities (e.g. sales organizations). This structure is an important basis for further configuration activities especially regarding process control (e.g. approval processes) as well as accounting and finance.

Edit Project Scope: First Implementation

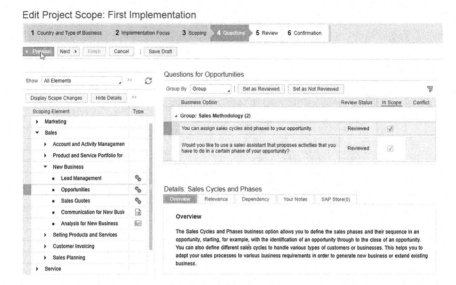

Fig. 3 A screenshot of the BAC showing an opportunity related question (© SAP AG)

The 'fine-tuning' as part of the activity list holds tasks with a graphical configuration dialog and a documentation. Although these tasks enable system configuration without any technical IT background, they require a certain business know-how and understanding regarding the effects on the system behavior in business processes. The tasks range from obligatory tasks mainly in finance and accounting, for instance the complex account determination, to optional tasks allowing changes in the behavior of the system, e.g. payment strategies (see Fig. 3), and also cover simple additions to the master data such as payment terms or special academic titles (Fig. 4).

An implementation project is carried out in a test environment, allowing test cases with actual business documents to be conducted. This also enables data migration into the test system to ensure the correctness of the data on top of the consistency checks performed in the migration assistant. Eventually, the configuration is completed in the test environment and the data migration files are released for the productive environment.

The configuration in the test environment is part of a 'solution profile' which contains the selections in the BAC and the configured tasks of the activity lists. When moving from test to a productive environment, the solution profile is applied to the productive system. Apart from a few task elements that require a configuration directly in the productive environment, all scoping decisions and configuration elements are retrieved automatically from the solution profile. The data migration with verified spreadsheets into the productive environment is another task in the go-live preparations.

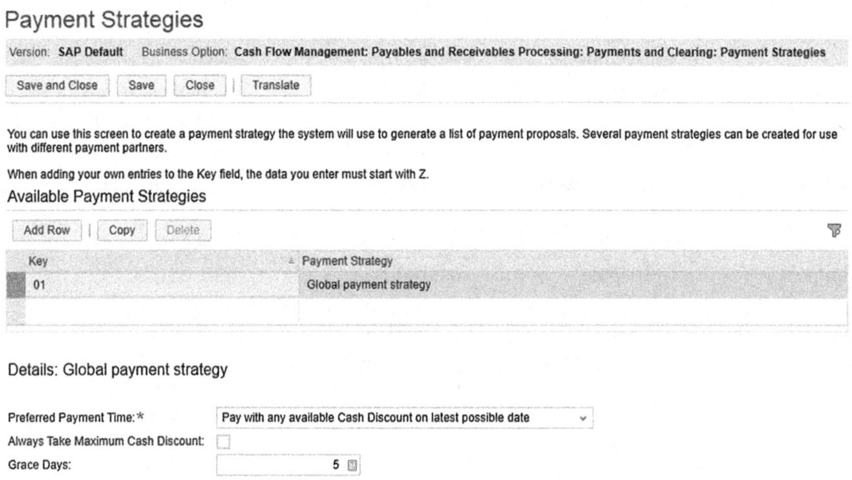

Payment Strategies

Version: **SAP Default**   Business Option: **Cash Flow Management: Payables and Receivables Processing: Payments and Clearing: Payment Strategies**

| Save and Close | Save | Close | | Translate |

You can use this screen to create a payment strategy the system will use to generate a list of payment proposals. Several payment strategies can be created for use with different payment partners.

When adding your own entries to the Key field, the data you enter must start with Z.

Available Payment Strategies

| Add Row | | Copy | Delete |

Key	⌃ Payment Strategy
01	Global payment strategy

Details: Global payment strategy

Preferred Payment Time: * | Pay with any available Cash Discount on latest possible date   ⌄ |

Always Take Maximum Cash Discount: ☐

Grace Days: | 5 🗒 |

Fig. 4 Configuration task regarding payment strategies in fine-tuning (© SAP AG)

After go-live the implementation project is closed as the configuration is considered finished. This results in a locked BAC but leaves fine-tuning elements such as the chart of accounts open for changes during productive use. In case adaptions to the BAC are required, the system offers the possibility to create a new implementation project that allows changes to be configured and applied either directly in the productive environment or with prior testing in a test environment.

Based on observations and description of the implementation methodology and the configuration in this chapter, the business-oriented configuration can be seen as a helpful contribution to ERP implementation projects. It enables a seamless connection between system configuration and project management phases and steps. Thus, it positively addresses several essential factors of success of a classical ERP implementation which suggest an expectation of shorter ERP implementation times.

Furthermore, the simplicity of the configuration and its elements from an IT perspective will also have positive effects on implementations for small and midsized companies as IT expertise is no longer required.

The following chapter analyses if these positive effects can actually be observed in real world projects. The chapter contains descriptions of specific implementation projects in small and midsized companies that implemented the cloud solution SAP Business ByDesign. The case studies try to show the implementation methodology as well as how the configuration was performed. Based on these case studies conclusions are drawn to investigate the effects further. This qualitative method was chosen as a quantitative analysis was not possible at the time of this paper. The results have a descriptive character but allow perceptions on the effectiveness of the business-oriented configuration methodology.

Table 2 Overview of the case studies in this paper

	Especcino	medpro	photaic
Employees	10 employees	35 employees	10 employees and 10 distribution partners
Sales volume	1 mio EUR	12 mio EUR	1 mio EUR
Industry	Retail, coffee and tea	Retail, healthcare	Retail, renewable energy
Project start	01.09.2011	01.09.2012	01.09.2013
Go-live	01.01.2012	01.01.2013	07.01.2014
Implemented business scenarios	Owner/executive, purchasing, accounting/finance, sales and marketing	Owner/executive, purchasing, accounting/finance, sales and marketing	Owner/executive, purchasing, accounting/finance, sales and marketing, service and support
Users	10 users	20 users	20 users
Implementation effort[a]	Medium	High	Little

[a] The implementation effort is derived from the sum of consultancy days by external partners during the implementation project. (little <= 50 days, medium <= 75 days, high > 75 days)

3   Business Cases Overview

Each of the case studies describes a specific implementation project of SAP Business ByDesign following the 'Launch' implementation methodology for SaaS products. Although being outlined in the same structure, each project shows its own characteristics as shown in Table 2.

3.1   Photaic AG

The photaic AG was founded in 2012 and focuses on decentralised power supply solutions. Its business includes the development of the solutions and the operation of a Pan-European distribution network with electricians and specialised partners.

The fast growing corporation had about ten employees and realized a sales volume of about one million Euro in the year 2013 with a distribution network of roughly ten sales representatives as well as various partners including electricians and wholesales partners.

Reasons for ERP

The existing IT infrastructure did not support the business processes of photaic and resulted in manual, partly handwritten, documents used to track orders along the fulfilment process. The service business, which started to evolve in 2013, relied on information from the order fulfilment process which was stored either in office documents or on paper and were not accessible when needed on short notice. With the growing business volume the requirements exceeded the capabilities of the existing solutions and photaic started looking for an integrated system.

The corporation decided to use SAP Business ByDesign because

- the implementation partner promised a fast implementation,
- the solutions is on-demand and due to this required no investments in IT infrastructure,
- all processes could be run in one integrated system equipped with in-memory technology providing enhanced and real-time reporting.

The Implementation Project at Photaic AG

To photaic and its management team it was very important that the go-live was on the 1st of January 2014. This date was clearly communicated and agreed upon with the implementation partner before the project started.

Project team.

Each party selected a project leader who was responsible for project management on their respective side. Photaic also nominated key users for the areas of order fulfilment, sales, procurement, after sales and services, accounting and controlling. The key users and the project leader remained in the daily business and compensated additional project work with overtime as far as necessary. A successful implementation was also part of their compensation relevant agreements of objectives. Additional workforce to assist in time-intensive work packages such as the data migration was provided by a third-party contractor.

System configuration.

The system scoping was done by the implementation partner based on the negotiated tender offer and an associated 'requirements workshop'. The fine-tuning of the system was carried out mainly by the key-users themselves after having participated in business area specific workshops held by the implementation partner. In general the workshops lasted for half a day and enabled key users to do configurations in their field of expertise based on their knowledge of the processes in the corporation and the input from the implementation partner. In case of questions the implementation partner was available and took a guiding role in this phase. A few complex configuration elements regarding the business processes in the system were done by the implementation partner.

Key users were able to configure master data for business partners, payment terms and sales master data such as customer groups and so on. The setup of the chart of accounts was mainly outsourced to the contractor as the capacities of the account key user were consumed by the daily business.

Data migration and go-live.

Despite an underestimated effort in data clean-up the data migration hardly interfered with neither the project plan nor the daily business of photaic as it was almost completely carried out by the contractor and only required coordinating activities from photaic. Apart from an agreed upon delay of one week due to an enterprise wide vacation period the project was on schedule and photaic had the go-live on the 7th of January 2014.

Key Learnings from the Implementation Project

Key users were able to compensate the additional implementation efforts to the daily business with overtime because of the assistance provided by the third-party contractor. This led to an increased coordination effort in general and a loss of know-how once the contractor was gone. This was especially hurtful in accounting as the key user changed after the go-live causing efforts of two additional days to train the new key user by the implementation partner.

The methodology used in this project addressed several success factors for ERP implementation. The workshops to perform the configuration by the key users resulted in a high level of involvement. Also, key users were able to provide additional background info and training to other users. The project-oriented methodology assisted in the planning and management of the project itself and also required an early involvement of the top management to define goals, scope and the organizational structure. The tight coupling between configuration and project management enabled a detailed progress analysis and allowed photaic to effectively outsource configuration elements and the data migration in case of capacity shortages. Due to the low technical know-how required to perform these tasks, the third-party contractor was able to perform tasks without any training efforts. Especially the data migration via office spreadsheets and a data import assistant including data quality checks proofed to be very beneficial in this process.

3.2   Medpro HandelsGmbH

The medpro HandelsGmbH is specialised in selling pharmaceutical products and dietary supplements. Their customer base ranges from pharmacies and doctors to consumers. They mainly operate in Austria and Germany.

The headquarters is located in Austria and medpro is operating a subsidiary in Germany. The enterprise had about 35 employees and achieved a sales volume of over 12 million EUR in 2013.

Reasons for ERP

Medpro was running a customer-specific legacy system which could be maintained only by one employee. The system lacked in reporting functionality due to missing integration into controlling and accounting. Cost transparency including stock prices of products and shipments costs were not available. Furthermore, the system was not seen as safe basis for the future development of the enterprise. Medpro decided to replace the legacy system with SAP Business ByDesign due to

- the software-as-a-service model,
- the continuous development of the solution by the software provider and the outlook towards new features enabling new business models for medpro in future releases,
- the streamline integration of their intercompany business processes,
- an integrated reporting accomplishing cost transparency along the business processes of medpro,
- the scalability of the system for future enhancements and integrations with third-party systems.

The Implementation Project at Medpro

Project team.
The project team consisted of three parties: medpro itself, an SAP partner and an external implementation partner company. The project leadership was equally distributed between medpro and the external implementation partner. As implementation style a go live assistance package was conducted, enabling a close cooperation between the medpro and the implementation partner while the SAP partner acted in a more supportive role.

System configuration.
The functional requirements were defined in workshops with the key users from procurement, sales, operations, logistics and finance. The bottom-up approach and early involvement of key users ensured the commitment from employees and department leaders. As key users were also responsible for system tests medpro ensured the quality of the implemented business processes. The scoping and complex configurations such as intercompany processes were mainly carried out by the implementation partner while the key users could implement business related configuration elements. Prior to the configuration key users attended specific workshops enabling them to do the business related configuration in the system.

Data migration and go-live.

The project timeline was tackled by a redesign of the complex drop-shipping process and a high amount of data for migration. The effort for data clean-up was underestimated and caused a delay of two weeks in the schedule. Effective configuration by key users and the implementation partner combined with overtime could later compensate the delay of the data migration and medpro could go live with SAP Business ByDesign as planned on the 1st of January 2013 after an intensive testing phase by the key users.

Key Learnings from the Implementation Project

The parties involved defined objectives early in the project and used the task-driven implementation methodology to distribute the tasks among them. The implementation partner could use their business know-how to transform functional requirements from key users into the system configuration. This was mainly possible because the configuration did not require technical know-how and enabled medpro to choose a consultancy they trusted. Furthermore, early involvement of key users in requirement definition workshops and further configuration steps ensured a high commitment and acceptance for the solution. This cooperative aspect of the implementation methodology was also welcomed by the top management. The close cooperation between key users and implementation partner proved especially helpful during the test phase when configuration adjustments became necessary. Due to the configuration workshops key users had a better understanding of the system and upcoming issues were quickly resolved.

Although the data migration was underestimated, the 'import assistant' allowed key users to verify the consistency of their data and revealed quality problems before the data was migrated into the system. As key users could resolve issues by themselves in the office spreadsheet documents, the delay was kept low. The tight implementation schedule challenged the project management and required a strict planning of the configuration which was achieved by an early scheduling of the key user workshops required by the implementation methodology. A strong reuse of standardized processes especially for the drop-shipping process addressed another success factor of ERP implementation by reengineering the process close to the system standard.

3.3   Especcino GmbH

"Enjoy the daily work" is the key philosophy of the Especcino GmbH which is the leading provider of coffee equipment and services for offices in Austria. They offer equipment, coffee and tea as packaged solutions for offices and restaurants.

The organization had about ten employees and achieved a sales volume of roughly one million Euro in 2012.

Reasons for ERP

The company grew over the past years due to increasing demand and success while the IT infrastructure was not adapted for business volume and number of transactions. This led to a mismatch between processes and IT which became more and more painful in daily business. Financial reporting was limited due to a lack of detailed transaction data and had a significant delay as data was not captured when the transaction happened. This also affected the warehouse management which often led to stock shortfalls or too high stock levels.

Especcino decided to implement SAP Business ByDesign because

- the solution integrated their business processes in one system,
- no new IT infrastructure was required,
- the solution enabled inventory optimization,
- financial key figures were available in real time and increased transparency of the business processes.

The Implementation Project at Especcino

Project team.
Especcino hired an external project leader to manage the project from the customer side while the implementation partner also provided a project manager. Other project members represented the management team of Especcino as well as key users and the tax adviser. The implementation was conducted in a coaching approach in which the implementation partner provided expert know-how to the external consultant and Especcino itself.

System configuration.
The external consultant and the implementation partner used the scoping tools to configure the system based on the requirements of Especcino. The implementation partner also conducted a prototype to discuss different ways of how to implement business processes with the customer. The configuration was mainly performed remotely in combination with on-site workshops with the users. The key users were responsible for easier business related configurations while the external consultant focused on process related fine-tuning activities. The designed solution was based on the standardized processes in the system to avoid customer-specific development efforts.

Data migration and go-live.
The data extraction from legacy systems and the data clearing were an intensive work stream along the implementation project. The actual migration with office spreadsheets, however, was not considered as an issue. The project was well planned and minor shifts in timelines counterbalanced with others. Before Especcino went live acceptance tests were performed by the users following test protocols and checklists. Eventually Especcino could go live as planned on the 1st of January 2012.

Key learnings from the implementation project.

The parties identified the close orientation on the standard processes as a key success factor for the implementation. Additionally, the external consultant proofed to be valuable by configuring business requirements from the customer into the system with the help of the implementation partner. The intensive involvement of the management through workshops also resulted in a clear commitment and secured a positive relationship with the tax adviser.

Key users were involved early in workshops and prototype assessment which facilitated them to perform in-depth integration tests based on test protocols before the go-live. Furthermore, data migration was seen not as a technical issue due to easy-to-use office spreadsheets. However, this tool could not improve the data quality and the unstructured form of data from the legacy systems.

Staying as close to standardized processes as possible enabled the training of the key users to be held with the learning content in the system itself and therefore did not require customized training efforts. The on-demand aspect of the system allowed the external consultant the implementation partner to work remotely and hence resulted in significant cost reductions due to saved travel costs.

According to the project leaders the implementation methodology and the built-in project-oriented aspects of the configuration highly contributed to the successful project management. In general at least four success factors listed in Table 1 were addressed in the implementation project.

This case study concludes this chapter which showed ERP implementations in small and midsized enterprises with a business-oriented configuration and the appropriate implementation methodology. The findings encourage positive effects of this innovation which are outlined and summarized in the conclusion.

4   Conclusion

Innovative ERP systems offer a new configuration methodology with a strong business orientation and claim to reduce implementation times. Traditionally, customizing led to many problems due to its high complexity and required a high level of expertise in different modules. Critical success factors of classical ERP implementations also show that organizational and managerial aspects have to be addressed during such projects.

An implementation and configuration methodology with a strong business orientation can be used to implement SAP Business ByDesign. The implementation comprises a phase model from a project management perspective combined with a business-oriented configuration that uses a 'Business Adaption Catalog' to define functional capacities and system behaviour. The configuration is performed in the system on an 'implementation project' by answering business questions in combination with completing guided tasks which also incorporate aspects of project management. In theory, the configuration methodology should contribute to decrease implementation times as it addresses several critical success factors of ERP implementations.

The following tables shows that this assumptions on theory were confirmed in a qualitative analysis of implementation case studies and pointed out positive effects of a business configuration methodology on the critical success factors. The ('+') symbol indicates that the mentioned positive effects were observed in a case study and were related to the introduced concept of a business configuration. In case either the effect or a clear correlation were not identified, the sign (' ~ ') was used.

As Table 3 indicates the key challenges in ERP implementation are shifting as innovative configuration methodologies emerge. The configuration of an ERP system is aligned with project management and can be executed faster than before even without IT expertise. The processes are closer to standard which reduces flexibility for the enterprises but also promotes the use of standardized support processes. The standardization also lowers complexity and hence implementation projects require less specialized consultants. These findings suggest ERP systems are becoming more attractive to small and midsized enterprises as shorter and less complex implementations reduce the risks for these organizations.

Since the number of overall implementations of SaaS systems like SAP's Business byDesign is still small, the method of qualitative analysis seems to be

Table 3 Effects on critical success factors of ERP implementation

Critical success factor	Positive effects observed in case studies	M	P	E
Involvement and training of users	Workshops are used to involve key users early and also to take over some configuration tasks	+	+	+
Project management	System configuration includes project management activities	+	+	+
Commitment of top management	Top management is involved early	~	~	+
Clearly formulated project objectives	Implementation methodology requires a definition of the objectives and the scope in the beginning	~	~	~
Method of implementation approach	The approach follows a SaaS implementation methodology	+	+	+
Technical requirements	No IT expertise is needed due to a business-oriented configuration. Infrastructure is required due to an on demand system	+	+	+
Risk of consultancy	Simpler configuration reduces the risk of consultancy	~+	+	~+
Reorganization of business processes	Less customization and high reuse of standard business processes but flexibility is limited	~	~	+
Time and resource management	Resources can be used more flexible and hence support tight schedules	~	+	~
Contract drafting	Early scope definitions could benefit the contract drafting process	~	~	~

[a]M, P and E refer to the case studies (medpro, photaic, and Especcino)

appropriate for first research activities in this field. In future, further quantitative research on ERP SaaS implementations should be conducted to analyze overall effects on ERP implementations and to prove the applicability of Enterprise Resource Planning systems for small and medium enterprises.

References

1. Eggert, S., Stritzel, M.: 92 ERP-Systeme im direkten Vergleich: Mobile ERP, Funktionen und die Trends 2014. ERP Manag 1/2014, 43–44 (2014)
2. Weisbecker, A.: Neue Chancen für den Mittelstand. HMD—Praxis der Wirtschaftsinformatik 285, 6–19 (2012)
3. Hufgard, A., Krüger, S: SAP Business ByDesign: Geschäftsprozesse, Technologie und Implementierung anschaulich erklärt. Galileo Press, Bonn (2011)
4. Von Arb, R.: Vorgehensweisen und Erfahrungen bei der Einführung von Enterprise Management Systemen dargestellt am Beispiel von SAP R/3. Bern (1997)
5. Gerhardter, A., Ortner, W.: Flexibility and improved resource utilization through cloud based ERP systems—critical success factors of SaaS solutions in SME (2012)
6. Hesseler, M., Görtz, M.: Basiswissen ERP-Systeme, Witten (2007)
7. Schumann, M.: Betriebliche Nutzeffekte und Strategiebeiträge der großintegrierten Informationsverarbeitung, Berlin (1992)
8. Tschandl, M., Ortner, W.: Effizienz betrieblicher Informationssysteme, 1. Auflage, Graz (2004)
9. Mertens, P.: Integrierte Informationsverarbeitung, vol. 17. Auflage, Wiesbaden (2009)
10. Grochla, E.: Integrierte Gesamtmodelle der Datenverarbeitung—Entwicklung und Anwendung des Kölner Integrationsmodells (KIM), München (1974)
11. Scheer, A.: Schnittstellen zwischen betriebswirtschaftlicher und technischer Datenverarbeitung in der Fabrik der Zukunft, Saarbrücken (1984)
12. Thomé, R., Hufgard, A.: Continuous System Engineering—Entdeckung der Standardsoftware als Organisator, Würzburg (1997)
13. Credé, H., Gralsund, K., Petri, M.: R/3-Einführung: Operation am offenen Herzen, Computerwoche (1997) (online)
14. Davenport, T.: Paßt ihr Unternehmen zur Software. Harv. Bus. Manager 2, 89–99 (1999)
15. Gerhardter, A.: Implementierung von ERP Systemen für kleine und mittelständische Unternehmen im Wandel der Zeit. Bachelorarbeit an der FH Joanneum, Kapfenberg (2011)
16. Blume, A.: Projektkompass SAP: Arbeitsorientierte Planungshilfen für die erfolgreiche Einführung von SAP-Software, vol. 3. Auflabe, Vieweg & Sohn, Braunschweig/Wiesbaden (1997)
17. Brand, H.: SAP R/3 Einführung mit ASAP: Technische Implementierung von SAP R/3 planen und realisieren, Addison Weslay Longman, Bonn (1999)
18. Umble, E., Hadt, R., Umble, M.: Enterprise Resource Planning: Implementation procedures and critical factors of success. Eur. J. Oper. Res. Heft 146, 241–257 (2003)
19. Esteves, J., Pastos, J.: A Critical success factor's relevance model for SAP implementation project. In: Lau, L. (ed.): Managing Business with SAP: Planning, Implementation and Evaluation, pp. 240–261. Idea Group, London (2005)
20. Siegenthaler, M., Schmid, C.: ERP für KMU. Praxisleitfaden: kurz & prägnant, Rheinfelden/Schweiz, BPX-Edition, 2006
21. Ciecko, D.: SAP Launch, https://wiki.sme.sap.com/wiki/display/AMI/SAP+Launch

ERP-Adoption Within SME—Challenging the Existing Body of Knowledge with a Recent Case

Frederik Kramer, Thomas Rehn, Markus Schneider and Klaus Turowski

Abstract This paper analyses and harmonizes the existing body of literature concerning enterprise resource planning system (ERP) adoption in small and medium-sized enterprises (SME). It conducts a single case study focused on challenging existing knowledge in a the rather scarce field of scientific research. We found the importance of success factors such as the "project champion", proper "project/change management" and "strong partnership" as well as risk such as "inadequate training and instruction" or "low key-user involvement" supported. Additionally our case further unveiled additional previously not mentioned success factors/risk, such as the "flexibility" provided by Open Source Software, "poorly specified legacy applications and interfaces" and "inadequate user acceptance and end-to-end testing"

Keywords ERP-adoption · Case study · Open source software · Cloud computing

F. Kramer (✉) · K. Turowski
Magdeburg Research and Competence Cluster (MRCC),
Otto-von-Guericke-University, Magdeburg, Germany
e-mail: frederik.kramer@ovgu.de
URL: http://www.mrcc.eu/

K. Turowski
e-mail: klaus.turowski@ovgu.de
URL: http://www.mrcc.eu/

T. Rehn · M. Schneider
initOS GmbH & Co. KG, Magdeburg, Germany
e-mail: thomas.rehn@initos.com
URL: http://blog.initos.com/

M. Schneider
e-mail: markus.schneider@initos.com
URL: http://blog.initos.com/

© Springer International Publishing Switzerland 2016   41
F. Piazolo and M. Felderer (eds.), *Multidimensional Views on Enterprise
Information Systems*, Lecture Notes in Information Systems and Organisation 12,
DOI 10.1007/978-3-319-27043-2_4

1   Introduction

Even if small and medium-sized enterprises (SME) already leverage IT to sustain in global markets, business applications continuously gain importance [1]. SME are different from large enterprises in many aspects. For example, it is significantly harder for them to gather equity or loans [2]. The scarcity of financial as well as personal resources render them special [2]. Furthermore, they are delineated by their operative focus [3]. The vast majority of SME is driven by entrepreneurs. Entrepreneurs are people that invest their own money, take a personal risk and are mostly liable for business operations [4]. These three aspects are required by many SME definitions such as the ones of the Institut für Mittelstandsforschung (IfM) ind Bonn or the one of the European Commission.

Due to the substantial difference between SME and large enterprises the body of knowledge on the successful adoption and implementation of business applications in large enterprises cannot directly be applied to SME. Enterprise Resource Planning (ERP) applications have generally acknowledges as something like the blueprint of complex business applications. The abstract requirement of such systems is to maintain business operations by supporting the horizontal business processes in one integrated business application. Although ERP are commonly referred to as "standard applications" their implementation usually qualify very complex projects.

Whereas the research on ERP systems, their adoption and the success factors of their implementation in large enterprises has been fueling academia since the early 1980s, research on its adoption in SME is still relatively scarce. This paper contributes to the body of knowledge in two ways. First it summarizes the research on ERP-system adoption and links that to the smaller portion of it that explicitly deals with SME. Second it contrasts the general findings with a single case scenario of an ERP implementation recently conducted with a small entrepreneurial SME in southern Germany.

2   Research Method and Paper Flow

Within this contribution a literature meta-study is being conducted [5]. For that purpose the body of knowledge on ERP-implementation success in large enterprises and SME is being revised and harmonized firstly. Secondly a case study of an ERP-implementation in an entrepreneurial SME in southern Germany is being thoroughly analyzed with regards to this consolidated perspective. The case study results are being used to challenge this actual body of knowledge. Finally as summary of findings together with an outlook on future research objectives rounds the paper up.

3   On the History of IT Success

During the late 1970s and early 1980s it became evident that capital expenditures on information technology (IT) had largely grown. Together with the increased expenditures the question on the factors framing their success arose. The term critical success factors (CSF) first appeared in an article by Rockart [6]. During the late 1980s and the early 1990s scientist, such as Brynjolfsson [7], became aware of the fact that expenditures on IT did not have the direct impact on productivity they had previously expected.

Brynjolfsson argued that this "productivity paradox" most probably existed because improvements could in most cases only be measured indirectly. In this context qualitative improvements such as better running and new business processes were mentioned. Often these improvement were only visible after a certain time delay. Brynjolfssons interpretation of the productivity paradox was mostly accepted amongst scholars across the world.

This time falls in conjunction with the success of standard applications such as SAP's famous R/3 system. Further on scientist rather focused on indirect quality measures linked to new businesses processes as well as improved efficiency of existing business processes while applying IT [8]. Ongoing efforts to standardize IT, such as for example standard enterprise resource planning systems, let Carr to argue on the evaporated differentiation potential of IT in its famous 2003 article entitled "IT doesn't matter" [9].

4   Success Framing Conditions of ERP Adoption

As already mentioned implementation of ERP-systems is known as one of the most critical IT endeavors of enterprises. This fact does not differ amongst large enterprises and SME [10]. Whereas large enterprises usually invest up to several -even hundreds of- millions into adoption and maintenance of ERP-systems, SME usually invest between several thousands and more than 100,000 Euro. Snider et al. claim that the investment into ERP-adoption were between 0.4 and 3.0 % of the annual turn over [11]. Owing to the German SME structure this would make up an average 45,000 Euro investment [12]. To both company types a failure would cause a substantial thread, however. This is because in both cases the sheer amount of money invested, relative to the annual turnover, is usually large.

In order to to facilitate our research we searched for high-quality journal publications and conference proceedings that had both keywords "ERP" and "SME" in either their title, abstract or keywords. After a first cleaning iteration we found the following eight papers relevant for our research [10, 11, 13–18]. After reading them entirely we added further papers to our investigation. For that purpose we mostly considered publications on ERP adoption from the larger body of enterprise adoption as they were linked in one of the initial papers. By doing so we came up

Table 1 Papers analyzed throughout this research

Author(s)	Applied research method(s)	SME specific
Motwani et al. [19]	Case Study Research	No
Moon [21]	Literature Review	No
Aloini et al. [20]	Literature Review	No
Skok and Legge [22]	Case Study Research	No
Fisher et al. [23]	Data Envelopment Analysis (DEA)	No
Deltour [13]	Quantiative Research	Yes
Snider et al. [11]	Case Study Research	Yes
Zach [14]	Case Study Research	Yes
Huq and Shah [15]	Case Study Research	Yes
Hustad and Olsen [16]	Case Study Research	Yes
Loh and Koh [17]	Literature Review and Interviews	Yes
Malhotra and Temponi [18]	Literature Review	Yes
Poba-Nzaou and Raymond [10]	Case Study Research	Yes

with following additional references [19–23]. The total set of analyzed papers together with its authors and the applied research method is shown in Table 1.

By reviewing the aforementioned body of knowledge we identified three major research objectives. One research objective is the **critical success factors** shaping ERP-adoption [11, 13, 14, 19], another is investigating the inherent **risk** [10, 13, 19] and the third is concerned with the **procedures of ERP-adoption** [16, 18, 19]. Last but not least we found interesting meta information on the ERP-adoption especially from those publications that conducted case study based research [13, 15, 19].

4.1 Critical Success Factors

Motwani et al. [19] found out that the following factors were relevant success factors for the investigated cases:

- Change Management
- Planning and execution
- Project Management
- Processes and system integrity
- Business plan and vision
- Collaboration between vendor and customer
- Project monitoring

Deltour showed that **external help** as well as the **individual capabilities of the external provider** were relevant for project success [13]. Deltour also found **change management** to be relevant for project success. He further pointed out that the shorter the projects were the more successful they were [13]. In that sense the

duration of the project is a success factor. Snider et al. distinguish success factors in different project phases, namely the pre-planning, the implementation and the project post-analysis phase [11]. Additionally to the aforementioned factors the authors found

- Strategic vision
- ERP fit
- Top management support
- Communication
- Business process optimization
- Training
- Internal implementation resource
- Performance measurement

relevant for project success. Zach complements the body of knowledge on success factors by stating that, due to the lack of strategic vision, rather short term **system and information quality** outcomes played a more important role than individual or organizational outcomes. In that sense ERP-systems had more often been employed to get rid of legacy systems, than as a result of strategic vision [14]. This is well in line with the generally observed lack of strategic planning within SME [24].

4.2 Risk

Poba-Nzaou and Raymond conducted a multiple case study on risk classification and risk management with ERP-adopting SME. The authors classified risk into one of seven risk dimensions as follows:

- Organizational risk
- Technological risk
- Business risk
- Financial risk
- Contractual risk
- Entrepreneurial risk
- Legal risk

By investigating the means of risk mitigation, the authors found out, that SME adhered to certain principles, policies and practices. For instance, all the four investigated cases made sure that the system was properly adapted to the organization (not vice versa). This principle has been found to reduce organizational as well as business risk. End-user involvement was also employed by all four cases and found to have positive effect on mitigating the same risk dimensions [10]. Aloini et al. by conducting a comprehensive literature analysis found 19 relevant risks in total [20]. The most often cited ones together with the project phase in which the appear are shown in Table 2.

Table 2 Top 10 risks encountered in ERP-adoption projects according to Aloini et al. [20]

Risk	Life cycle phase
Inadequate ERP selection	Concept/selection
Ineffective strategic thinking and planning strategic	Concept/strategic planning
Ineffective project management techniques	Implementation/deployment
Bad managerial conduction	Concept/strategic planning
Inadequate change management	Implementation/integration
Inadequate training and instruction	Implementation/integration
Poor project team skills	Concept/selection
Inadequate BPR	Concept/strategic planning
Low top management involvement	Concept/strategic planning
Low key user involvement	Concept/selection

4.3 Planning Methodology

Hustad and Olsen did an in-depth single case analysis of a Norwegian retail company and found out that the SME had applied an elaborated planning methodology coming up with six potential implementation candidates. Unlike most cases that we have seen so far, the entrepreneur in case of Hustad and Olsen's research was very eager to learn more about the ERP market and participated in a topic-related annual conference for several years.

The entrepreneur was very concerned about the information asymmetry that exists between vendor and customer. The authors stated that consultancy (especially independent from the vendor/integrator) is very important throughout the entire planning as well as the project implementation phase [16]. This finding is well in line with the claims of Skok and Legge [22]. However, as Hustad and Olsen further found out consultants often follow their own plans framing an agency problem between the customer and the consultant.

Malhotra and Temponi put together an ERP framework consisting of 6 consecutive steps as follows [18]:

- Program team structure
- Implementation strategy
- Transition technique
- Database conversion strategy
- Risk management strategy
- Change management strategy

The authors state a **heavyweight program team structure** would be most suitable for SME's because the project manager can combine the role of the projects' major advocate (i.e. project champion [19]) and cover the change manager role simultaneously [18]. The authors further suggest a **partner implementation strategy** since this would allow an optimal split of responsibilities. As for the transition technique the authors suggest a **phased implementation** since that leaves time also to supply chain partners to develop necessary interfaces [18].

Due to the complexity and budget constraints, **manual database transition** is suggested to be the most efficient strategy for SME, because data cleaning and training can be done underway and it is generally recognized to be cheaper. As for risk mitigation a well elaborated selection process, including a careful analysis of alternatives, should be conducted according to the authors. Finally, a clear vision, together with a strong internal project champion and proper communication, assures the appropriate change management.

5 Case Study

We conducted a case study within a small entrepreneurial company. The case study took place between the last quarter of 2013 and ended quite recently before writing this paper. The company is a young entrepreneurial company. It started its operation in mid-2011 with a team of three people and grew quite rapidly throughout 2012 and 2013 to actually reach a headcount of roughly 35 employees. It quite recently surpassed the annual forecasted turnover of 10 Mio. Euro. The company since its inception extensively uses open source software and cloud computing.

After initially starting with private equity, the company received three rounds of venture capital (VC) funding; first, from a group of peers that contributed own equity, and more recently from a well-known family office. The company offers around 10,000 different products in five categories. Its focus group is young women between 18 and 35 years of age. The company operates a special-interest shop and belongs to the food industry.

5.1 Outset of the Project

The company since its inception had already used a Software as a Service (SaaS) based ERP-system named Actindo. Actindo has been named the ERP-system of the year 2012 by the Potsdam located Center of Enterprise Research. Actindo as a SaaS offering has a few compelling advantages, which likely make it a reasonable choice for small trading companies. Some of these advantages are:

- Small monthly fee, starting at 29 Euro per month
- Web-based user interface (based on ExtJS, improves accessibility)
- Almost no investment for setup and customizing
- Out-of-the box integration with marketplaces such as eBay and Amazon
- Paypal and banking integration
- TÜV-certification

In the setup of our case study Actindo has been used together with Magento. Magento is an e-commerce solution and as such the initially most important system of an e-commerce startup. Therefore Magento holds the primary product catalog, the availability on stock and the most important base data (i.e. customer data) as well as all the most important transactional data (orders, invoices). What e-commerce applications are traditionally bad at/not made for, is the baseline requirements of transaction logic required to keep the general ledger and legal accounting in good shape as well as the downstream supply chain and order fulfillment.

Also business reporting and stock management is not a well known strength of e-commerce platforms such as Magento. At the time the company was relatively small (with just a few to 100 orders a day) the transactional data (i.e. order lines) and base data (i.e. customer data) was replicated into Actindo in order to keep the general ledger there and produce the invoices. Since Actindo is a SaaS cloud offering, the only viable solution to do so, was to upgrade Actindo to the largest available package (priced at around 500 Euro a month), because the maximum amount of web service calls required this.

Even tough that had been done, the interface remained problematic and a single point of failure. The data could only be replicated from Magento to Actindo by manually invoking the replication, since Actindo did not provide a solution to run this task automatically.

5.2 Major Pain Points

Even in set-ups were strategic planning is more elaborated than concluded in literature, and also in the majority of cases we have investigated over the years switching cost may prohibit the change of ERP-systems [25]. The project that we have investigated is no exception. Throughout the year 2013, as the company grew rapidly and reached on average more than 500 sales per day, it became obvious that the interface between Actindo and Magento had become a substantial threat.

Not only that the interface was not capable of delivering the estimated transactional performance and scaling expectations, there were simply some required functions that did not work. For example, a full and valid log of financial transactions could not be obtained from the user interface in a consistent way. This fundamental requirement of a standard ERP-system accounted for multiple iterations with the support team and their direct database access. It was more than obvious that Actindo was not made for this kind of individual flexibility requirements.

For example the customer operates three different stock locations and wanted to instantiate a constraint-based picking logic. Actindo does not provide any method to do so. Due to its nature of a multi-tenant, SaaS-based Cloud Offering, customer-specific changes were mostly out of scope of Actindo's strategy. Even a direct link between the entrepreneur of the customer and the CEO of Actindo did not provide an acceptable and timely solution. The aforementioned issues, however, just demarcate the tip of the iceberg.

5.3 System Alternatives

Even if good practice in large enterprises and also seen as major risk in literature (see Table 2) an elaborated selection process had not been conducted in order to select the new ERP-system to go with. Instead, the entrepreneur favored and open source based approach. This was mostly the case because the flexibility that Magento offered throughout the growth phase of the company, combined with the solution competence of the implementation partner, had always been superior to what the entrepreneur heard from other e-commerce ventures in the area.

In order to be able to compare system alternatives the venture capital company in preparation of the board decision asked a local system integrator of ABAS for a first quotation. This was more considered the threshold investment than a viable solution, because it did not go into detail with process analysis and requirements engineering. After all the solution the entrepreneur favored was based on open source software.

Amongst various other open source ERP-solutions such as Apache OFBiz, Adempiere and Openbravo, OpenERP or Odoo as it is now named has gained the most momentum, recently. With more than 2 million users and over 500 implementation partners across the globe[1] it reached the largest market penetration amongst the open source based solutions. OpenERP S.A. the company behind Odoo has earned prices from technology analysts such as Ernst & Young and Deloitte in 2012 and 2013.[2] Moreover various success stories have already proven the capability to integrate Odoo with Magento.[3]

Last but not least the implementation partner of the company had considerable experience with Odoo implementations, which was seen as a very important factor by both the VC and the entrepreneur and became at least a subjective decision criteria, hence.

5.4 Project Conditions

At the beginning of the migration project the implementation partner and the entrepreneur set together to discuss potential alternative scenarios to replace the existing ERP-system. It was clear to both parties that Actindo was no longer capable to scale and did not deliver the required grade of flexibility for future growth. For both partners it was also clear, however, that this project could only be succeeding, if both would take joint responsibility in terms of transparent planning, budgeting and risk.

---

[1]see http://www.odoo.com for details.

[2]see   https://www.odoo.com/blog/odoo-news-5/post/three-awards-for-openerp-in-2013-139   for details.

[3]see http://odoo-magento-connector.com/.

Referring to risk it was moreover clear that failure to deliver would have caused substantial threats to the entrepreneurs' as well as the implementation partners' well-going. Both unanimously agreed that the project could not contain any risk buffer (in terms of budget) and any non-necessary (i.e. nice-to-have) features. Both partners also agreed that this project could only be initiated due to prior experience and based on a solid long-term partnership that connected the partners. The entire project was hence framed by strong entrepreneurial will on both sides and not by well-balanced cost/risk analysis considerations and/or contracts.

5.5   *Requirements Gathering*

Throughout the planning of the project, requirements engineering was done primarily by asking key users on their requirements with regards to their daily work. This structured gathering process was done by supervising key users while conducting their daily business using Actindo and letting them also focus on the weaknesses of the system handling.

This task was mostly done by the entrepreneur himself. During the project kick-off meeting it had been decided to prepare visual models of the main business processes. These were modeled as business process modeling notation representations (BPMN) using the on-line modeling toolkit at http://www.draw.io. An example of this work is shown in Fig. 1.

In several iterations, containing a full two-day workshop the planning team (principal consultant, development leader, entrepreneur) together came up with a

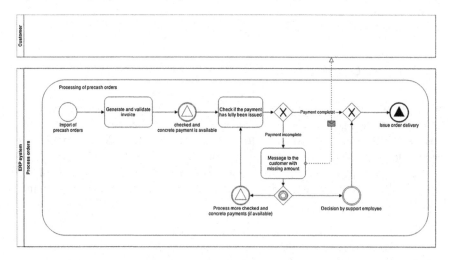

Fig. 1 Pre-cash order processing BPMN-model

list of 70 fundamental requirements. The project plan was subsequently divided into the following three major phases:

- Phase 0: Project planning (3 milestones)
- Phase 1: Implementation Core Features (16 milestones, 64 requirements)
- Phase 2: Implementation Extensions (6 milestones)

5.6 Implementation

Phase 0 contained all planning and modeling activities, that needed to take place in preparation for implementing the core features (Phase 1). Phase 2 contained major extensions that are primarily focusing on fully automating the supply chain. The main development and implementation phase took place between February 2014 and August 2014 (end of Phase 1).

The project had been estimated at roughly 1200 man hours (including project management and developer testing activities). The amount of work actually spent until the day of the migration was almost 1600 man hours. The overspending of more than 30 % was primarily caused by the fact that some of the Phase 2 features had been already implemented in Phase 1 in order to achieve a higher grade of automation earlier in the project. Additionally diverse marketing activities caused a significantly higher workload at the customer side. This in turn resulted in significantly less user testing (that was planned to be entirely done by the customers staff).

Less user testing and training activities caused significant communication overheads and nearly doubled efforts in some particular implementation activities. It also delayed the migration by more than a month.

6 Interpretation of Case Findings and Outlook

During the case investigation of this case study Phase 0 and Phase 1 have been performed successfully. Additionally some of the automation features have been already implemented in Phase 1. Since Phase 2 mostly contained improvements that were focusing on faster returns, they were not entirely required and planned to be implemented for the initial migration. Even if previously known and determined as being very risky, change management and training were neither added on the project road map nor were these items budgeted. Testing, according to the plan, was planned to be almost entirely done by the customers' own employees which in the end needed significant support by the implementation partner in terms of skill and human resources. This was all decided, because the project had to fulfill all Phase 1 requirements under a certain, more political, budget constraint.

Even if some intended (additional features, functional changes) as well as unintended changes (testing activities, change management) to the project roadmap caused a 33 % overspending for Phase 0 and Phase 1, the project up to this point was unanimously seen as a success. It is one of the largest reported ERP-migration projects from an entry-scale SaaS cloud offering to the leading open source ERP-system Odoo (formerly known as OpenERP).[4] More than 100,000 customer data sets, 15,000 product data sets (including supplier information) and more than 200,000 sale orders have been migrated from Actindo to Odoo on Friday, 29th of August 2014. The entire data migration process took more than three full days of processing.[5] Thanks to good design, migration planning and testing the migration procedure itself has been started asynchronously the Wednesday before the actual migration date (i.e. migration of end user operations). Odoo is on full operation since day one. The project team did not experience any critical downtime, impacting the main business of the customer. Several hundreds of sale orders are processed per day since that time. Due to the advanced picking logic and payment clearance[6] an automátion grade larger than 95 % has been achieved. More than one full-time equivalent (FTE) is saved since than. Also Sunday work is no longer necessary.

In summary our case provided evidence, that the following factors derived from literature indeed seemed to play an important role towards project success:

- Project champion
- The collaboration between the implementation partner and the customer
- Thorough planning and good project management
- Full commitment of all involved parties

We also found support that the following items were indeed major risks:

- Wrong/inadequate change management
- Inadequate training and instruction
- Low key user involvement (even if experienced primarily within the implementation phase)

Additional to the investigated literature we found the following issues to be very important:

- The degree of flexibility that is provided by open source software
- Community code and support as an important source of innovation, discussion and solution speed (this played a major role in solving problems with brutto/netto pricing differences of the two involved major systems)
- Poor specification of legacy applications and interfaces
- Inadequate user acceptance and end-to-end testing
- Inadequate/not existing load scenario and scaling test (this was left out for budgeting constraints as well)

---

[4]see www.odoo.com for details.

[5]from the first historic customer dataset to the most recent sale order.

[6]feature from Phase 2 that was already implemented in Phase 1.

Especially with regard to the findings of Poba-Nzaou and Raymond [10], we found that open source software, since it can be changed in literally any imaginable way, might mitigate the organizational as well as business risk dimension significantly. However, this "changeability" might cause for higher maintenance cost in later phases of the project life cycle or the requirement to disclose even the most competitive changes to the public space (due to the specific copy-left constraints of certain Open Source licenses, such as the GPL).

This paper, to our best knowledge, is the only single case analysis of an ERP-migration project from a SaaS-based cloud offering to a hosted open source ERP-solution. The projects' framing conditions are somewhat special and might call for idiosyncrasy therefore. First, not every good and potentially well-fitting ERP-system is open source software or delivered as SaaS-based Cloud offering. The majority indeed are on-premise proprietary ERP-Solutions such as SAP, Navision, Sage etc. Second the fact that Actindo isn't the only SaaS offering and its bad interface capability was not compared with other SaaS solutions does not allow generic claims in favor or against Cloud SaaS offerings.

However, we are confident that our case, while supporting many findings from already existing literature unveiled additional and potentially very important findings. For example we believe that inadequate user acceptance and end-to-end testing and poor specification of legacy applications might become much more important for SME in the future since ever more users and legacy applications need to be connected throughout the ERP-projects of SME. This to our point of view is inevitable owing to the ever faster pace of global market change.

References

1. Cole, T.: Unternehmen 2020 Das Internet War Erst Der Anfang. Hanser (2010)
2. Calcagnini, G., Favaretto, I. Calcagnini, G., Favaretto, I. (eds.): The Economics of Small Business an International Perspective. Physica Springer Distributor (2010)
3. Hunter, M.G., Diochon, M., Pugsley, D., Wright, B., Idea Group Publishing, H. (ed.): Managing Information Technology in Small Business Challenges and Solutions Unique Challenges fos Small Business Adoption of Information Technology: The Case of the Nova Scotia Ten Burgess, S, pp. 98–117 (2002)
4. Kayser, G., Schweinsberg, K., Schulz, C.: MIND 2004—Der MIttelstand in Deutschland: Wachsen aus eigener Kraft Gruner+Jahr AG & Co KG, Wirtschaftspresse Kln, Deutscher Sparkassen- und Giroverband (DSGV), Berlin (2004)
5. Webster, J., Watson, R.T.: Analyzing the past to prepare for the future: writing a literature review. MIS Q. **26**(2), xiii–xxiii (2002)
6. Rockart, J.F.: Chief executives define their own data needs. Harv. Bus. Rev. **57**, 81–93 (1979)
7. Brynjolfsson, E.: The productivity paradox of information technology. Commun. ACM. **36**, 66–77 (1993)
8. Hammer, M., Champy, J. Reengineering the corporation : A manifesto for business revolution. HarperBusiness (1993)
9. Carr, N.G.: IT doesn't matter. Harv. Bus. Rev. **5** (2003)
10. Poba-Nzaou, P., Raymond, L.: Managing ERP system risk in SMEs: a multiple case study. J. Inf. Technol. Assoc. Inf. Technol. Trust (2010)

11. Snider, B., da Silveira, G.J., Balakrishnan, J.: ERP implementation at SMEs: analysis of five canadian cases. Int. J. Oper. Prod. Manag. **29**, 4–29 (2009)
12. Kramer, F., Turowski, K.: Wie viel Agilität vertragen sie?. In: Proceedings der Wismarer Wirtschaftsinformatik Tage 2014, Wismar, 12–13 Juni 2014
13. Deltour, F.: ERP Project in Smes: a matter of risks, a matter of competencies. A quantitative analysis. In: Proceedings of the European Conference on Information Systems (2012)
14. Zach, O.: Exploring ERP system outcomes in SMEs: a multiple case study. In: Proceedings of the European Conference on Information Systems (2011)
15. Huq, N., Shah, S.M.A.: Why selecting an Open Source ERP over proprietary ERP? A focus on SMEs and suppliers perspective Japing. Int. Bus. Sch. (2010)
16. Hustad, E., Olsen, D.-H.: Exploring the ERP pre-implementation process in a small-and-medium-sized enterprise: a case study of a norwegian retail company. In: ECIS 2011 Proceedings (2011)
17. Loh, T.C., Koh, S.C.L.: Critical elements for a successful enterprise resource planning implementation in small-and medium-sized enterprises. Int. J. Prod. Res. **42**, 3433–3455 (2004)
18. Malhotra, R., Temponi, C.: Critical decisions for ERP integration: small business issues. Int. J. Inf. Manag. **30**, 28–37 (2010)
19. Motwani, J., Subramanian, R., Gopalakrishna, P.: Critical factors for successful erp implementation: exploratory findings from four case studies. Comput. Ind., Elsevier Science Publishers B. **56**, 529–544 (2005)
20. Aloini, D., Dulmin, R., Mininno, V.: Risk management in ERP project introduction: review of the literature. Inf. Manag. **44**(6), 547–567 (2007)
21. Moon, Y.B. Enterprise resource planning (ERP): a review of the literature. Int. J. Manag. Enterp. Dev. Inderscience **4**, 235 (2007)
22. Skok, W., Legge, M.: Evaluating enterprise resource planning (ERP) systems using an interpretive approach. Knowl. Process Manag. **9**(2), 72–82 (2002)
23. Fisher, D.M., Kiang, M.Y., Fisher, S.A., Chi, R.T.: Evaluating mid-level ERP software. J. Comput. Inf. Syst. **45**(1), 38–46 (2004)
24. Wang, C., Walker, E.A., Redmond, J.: Explaining the lack of strategic planning in smes: the importance of owner motivation. Int. J. Organ. Behav. **12**, 1–16 (2007)
25. Peltier, J. W., Zhao, Y. & Schibrowsky, J. A.: Technology adoption by small businesses: an exploratory study of the interrelationships of owner and environmental factors. Int. Small Bus. J. **30**, 406–431 (2012)

Challenge Detailed Planning in ERP

Norbert Obermayr

Abstract Each ERP-system plans very carefully, but determinate software plans with inaccurate data. The result is doubtful. This paper shows on why planning results are not very useful and how to manage uncertain data. Many companies use a capacity-planning with time-units in seconds, but the input-data only allows statements in hours. Future ERP-systems have to combine a learning process organisation with a personal leadership organisation to optimize the planning results and to achieve market close.

Keywords Deterministic planning under uncertainty · Data management · Unsafe to incorrect data · Learning processes

1 Introduction

The efficiency of a production company and therefore its competitiveness is determined in large part on the quality of the planning. Manufacturing planning and shop floor control are key functions of an ERP system. The functionality of the software can be adapted very well to the operational processes; data processing and thus also to the predictability of individual processes, however, depend on the data quality. Any software can reach just as good results as well the input data are. This paper mainly focuses on the input data and the impact is to be set when plan and reality diverge. The further remarks are always based on the focus of detailed planning.

The data for production planning is related to product- and production-data and also to order data. The product data are defined on the article master and the bill of

---

N. Obermayr (✉)
Dr. Obermayr GmbH, Himmelbergerstraße 3/10, Linz 4030, Austria
e-mail: n.obermayr@obermayr-ec.com

© Springer International Publishing Switzerland 2016   55
F. Piazolo and M. Felderer (eds.), *Multidimensional Views on Enterprise Information Systems*, Lecture Notes in Information Systems and Organisation 12, DOI 10.1007/978-3-319-27043-2_5

material no later than the time of order—apart from short-term changes in the phase of order. Depending on customer impact the standard products are long-term fixed data. For custom products, the data are often developed only after the order is placed. But at the time of detailed planning are primarily the product data in the form of master data and parts lists available.

The production data relate on the one hand to the specific production of an article in the form of work plans and on the other hand to the manufacturing system. The work plan provides information on what is to be produced as and where, and how long is the scheduled occupancy time. The information on the production system would provide information on the availability and performance. Although production data for the planning of each workshop control are critical, so still it must be noted that in many companies, these data are often just very inaccurate. The further implementation shall be addressed to the importance of the production data in the production planning and shop floor control.

The other planning data for the controller are determined by the customer on the order or on the production program. The order data are described on the product, the quantity and the delivery date. The contract value is true for the control no determining factor, but also gives information on material and labor inputs. Depending on the product and market the variance of the contract value may vary. The smaller the variance the easier is the ability to plan for the company. It becomes difficult for companies with very high variance because both the optimal supply of materials management as well as the optimal output suffer through a constant capacity utilization of the high variance.

2 Production Planning

The function of production planning is divided into sub-functions scheduling and capacity planning. The scheduling determines which shop order at what time and on what resources (workplace) is to be made (Fig. 1).

Capacity planning calculates the required occupation period for each workplace, and compares these capacity requirements in relation to the capacity stock. The data required for these functions come from the production master data, specifically from the workplace data, from the factory calendar, from the bill of material and the operation chart in connection with the order data (Fig. 2).

What are the challenges to the production planning? The main logistical key data is the delivery dependability. This ratio indicates how many orders were actually delivered to the agreed delivery date. The prerequisite for this is that at the time of production planning on the one hand the capacity situation is known and also that the processes and process times were correctly assessed. Here already are the first issues: the capacity requirements and thus the capacity utilization is determined by the target times of operations. A second problem is the scheduling. The occupancy time (scale bar in the Gantt chart) is determined by the schedule time. The temporal

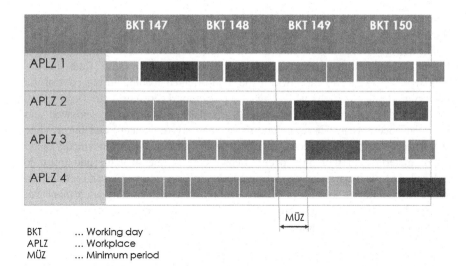

BKT   ... Working day
APLZ   ... Workplace
MÜZ   ... Minimum period

Fig. 1 Sequencing in detailed planning

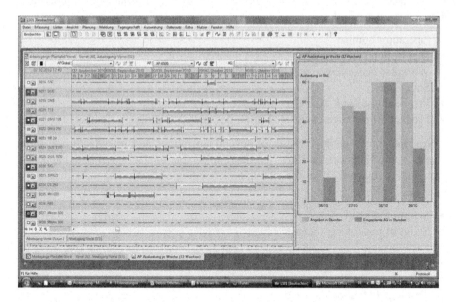

Fig. 2 Sequencing and capacity planning using the example of a control panel

sequence of operations is determined in many systems, using a running time factor.[1] This in turn is a function of the schedule time.

The delivery reliability depends in turn on the production cycle time. The longer the productions lead time the more jobs are at the same time in the workshop. According to the laws of the load-oriented manufacturing control the delivery reliability worsens while capacity utilization keeps constant.

The production main data are largely constant or are usually reviewed and redefined once a year. These include the availability (efficiency) and the average performance factor. The product configuration is determined deterministically in the bill of material and will only occur if an article is not available and must be replaced. The planning sheet indicates the individual operations for parts production and subassemblies as well as for final assembly. An analysis of the work plans can often be found that plan and reality differ considerable. These differences make the production planners hard time.

3   Problems at Operations Scheduling

A planning sheet (the movement data area) is divided into operations; the individual data fields in a record are:

- Operation number
- Description of operation
- Workplace/cost center (e.g. complemented with machine group)
- Setup-time
- Planned time (unit time t_U)
- Production resources and tools (tool, device, CNC program number)

An operation usually consists of several operations and manufacturing steps. A step "setup" and a second step "production" are per operation—if both happen—provided as standard. Take the example of "turning a shaft": The individual steps may be:

- Setup of several tools
- Setup of tensioning means
- Face turning
- Center drilling
- Turn the outer diameter
- Turning shaft shoulders 1 to n

In the example as shown are beside two setup-steps still 4 to n manufacturing operations cited. For each step personal and workplace-related schedule times are to create. A function "schedule time calculation" is only in very few ERP systems

---

[1]RTF = $(\sum\text{running time}/\sum\text{loading time})_{WP}$.

available. The plan time determination therefore usually takes place outside of an ERP system using Excel spreadsheet or by means of planned value tables. In rare cases, software for the planning period determination is used.

The practical experience shows that scheduled times stored in the planning sheet has a deviation of up to 200 %. But if these times are the basis for the scheduling, then the quality of the planning depends on the quality of the scheduled times. The problems of incorrect scheduling and incorrect capacity planning intensify exponentially; experienced workshop managers rely on their own experiences, rather than the detailed planning.

3.1   The Meaning of "Real" Target Times

Planning times differ from the actual times; this is normal within tolerable limits. However, do two fundamental questions:

- Why deviates from the schedule time of the actual time?
    - Is the scheduled time "wrong"? Or
    - Is in the work the respective performance level compared to the normal performance rate exceeded or not reached?

- What is different from this?
    - Are the mean values of the deviations too long, and how steep or flat is the distribution curve?
    - Are the mean values of the deviations too short, and how steep or flat is the distribution curve? (Fig. 3)

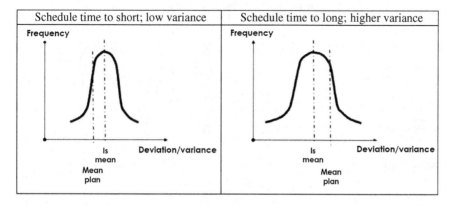

Fig. 3 Examples of distribution curves at inaccurate planned times

The plan will set a time based on normal capacity. Depending on the type of production and, depending on the guide, the actual performance to differ (measured as the related performance period value = time degree or as individual performance value = performance factor) of the normal workload. Additional performance in many ERP systems is taken into account in the form of a stored average performance factor. Reduced services are either a question of missing skills or lack of power will, and thus a question of leadership.

In many cases, the plan time calculation is inaccurate. It can be observed that within a company, the times either generally is rather too long or—which is the case more often—are too short. What are the consequences of inaccurate schedule times? (Fig. 4).

The more different the mean of the planned times from the mean of the actual times and the shallower the distribution curve of deviations the harder it is to plan ahead. It is expressed ultimately in the parameters of capacity utilization and timeliness (prompt delivery) from (Fig. 5):

An essential requirement in detailed planning is therefore the quality of the planning data. Not infrequently ERP systems work with minute units, while the accuracy of the planned times can be measured even in hour units. A study by a German consultancy firm shows that only 5 % of all scheduled times lie in a range of inaccuracy ≤ 10 % (Fig. 6).

What are the effects inaccurate schedule times?

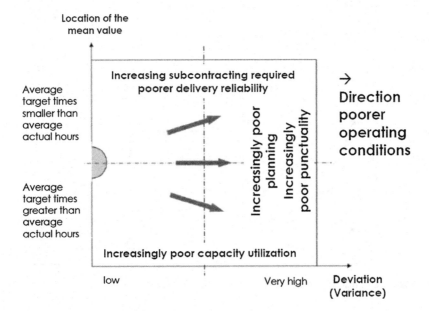

Fig. 4 Impact of inaccurate schedule times

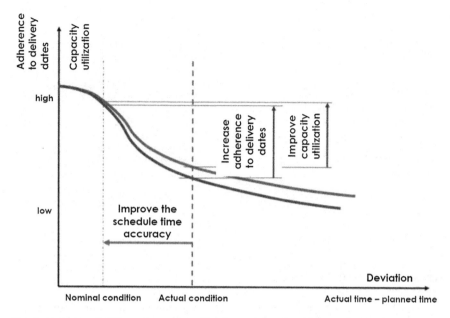

Fig. 5 Delivery reliability and capacity utilization as a function of time schedule deviations

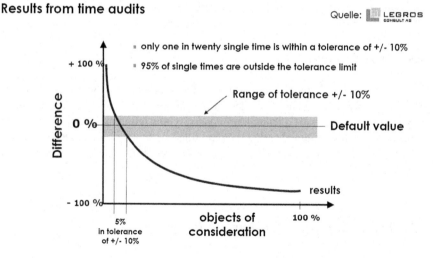

Fig. 6 Distribution curve of the discrepancies

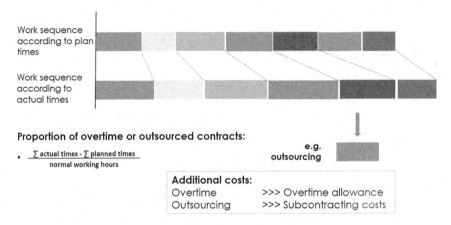

Fig. 7 Schedule times mostly too short

Schedule Times Mostly Too Short

In general, to plan short times have the effect that the individual operations ultimately can actually take longer than planned. This shifts the next step to give this
more time. This shift is extended from operation to operation. Ultimately need to be
done in overtime or subcontracting to maintain the planning individual operations.
Both are associated with additional costs (Fig. 7).

Schedule Times Mostly Too Long

Generally too long planned times have the effect that—not always available or not
yet available for subsequent jobs—depending on the load factor. This can result in
assignment gaps that have a reduction in capacity utilization as a result. If it comes
to large gaps before in practice that they are filled with other orders. Depending on
the availability of such contracts as it can but be shifts of the scheduled jobs
(Fig. 8).

3.2 The Importance of Complete Processes

In each production process and a number of logistical tasks must be completed in
addition to the value adding work. Very often these tasks are performed by the
operators of the machines. The times required for these tasks "go in", they are often
not taken into account. This essential process steps are not planned; the effect is the
same as that of too short (because not planned) scheduled times (Fig. 9).

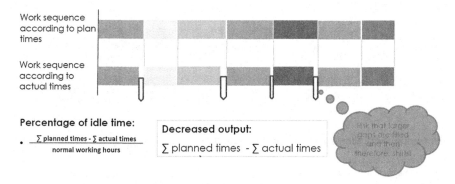

Fig. 8 Schedule times mostly too long

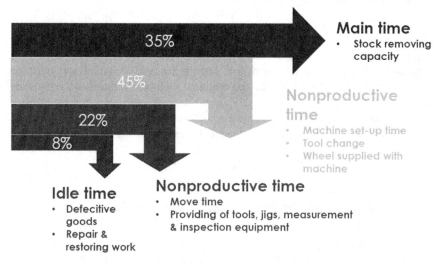

Fig. 9 Distribution of time units (example)

Depending on the manufacturing system, the number of non-value-adding productive time represents a very high percentage. The problem of the complete manufacturing process planning is that very often there is a discrepancy between the theoretical planning, carried out by a planner working in the office, and the operational reality. As in the workshops—if at all—only start and end times will be covered by the coats of the workshop orders also created no possibility for detecting complete sequences. This is also where no learning effect and the incomplete process planning is prolonged.

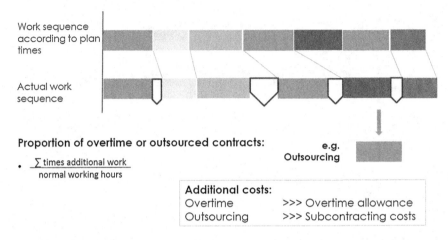

Fig. 10 Individual process steps are not planned

Even in companies with individual production there are standard recurring sequences with similar process steps. The task that arises from this is that the probability of occurrence and also how long it takes is recorded and must be provided for detailed planning. The conventional methods in the ERP systems are not sufficient (Fig. 10).

Incomplete scheduled processes have a similar effect as processes to plan short times. Unplanned operations must be inserted; then cause the displacement of the subsequent work with the already known effects.

3.3 The Importance of Proper Capacitance Values

The theoretical capacity is reduced by many more or less predictable events on available capacity. But even this capacity is often not available for production operations when unplanned downtime and production losses and additional expenses take away part of the available capacity (Fig. 11).

The workshop orders are assigned to individual workstations with their scheduled times. The inaccuracy of the order time now is superimposed on the inaccuracy of the capacitance values. The result is that the quality of the detailed planning can vary depending on the data accuracy to uselessness. Then it does not help when the best planning algorithms are mapped into the software.

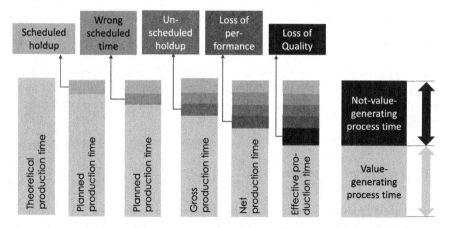

→ What can the causes of unplanned downtime be?

Fig. 11 Value-added production time and theoretical production time

4 Interim Conclusion

The quality of the detailed planning depends to a degree on the quality of the whole process with the "right" to budget time and actual available capacity. Would it be enough if these 3 conditions were fully met? Not at all. For it is in manufacturing operations to socio-technical systems; that is, man is an elusive deterministic factor. A "right" time plan for the employee "Huber" must be no "right" time plan for the employee "Smith". It depends on the ability of the employee and also on its disposition. Therefore, the plan times refer to a so-called "standard output"; this means that a skilled person can carry out the work over a long period of time. The actual time taken individually relative to budgeted time determines the level of performance.

This is yet another facet added: the level of performance than individual per-formance value for each procedure or time degree as an average over all ratios. Depending on the leadership of the enterprise shows that at a defined benefit plan management, the times can be achieved to a greater extent than if this is not the case. This also their specific environment plays a significant role. The factors influencing the management and the environment can be difficult displayed in one software. Maybe Fuzzy Logic can to offer a solution.

Achieving a high quality map data is not only a technical issue, but is also influenced by individual circumstances and is a matter of management.

5 What Can Solutions for More Effective Planning Data Be?

The assignment of units of capacity is determined by the process steps (operations) and the time required. Thus, the solution in the complete planning of all tasks must be both content and time. It is on the one hand a technical and on the other hand a personal-related (sociological) task.

5.1 Technical Solutions

The planned time consist of the machine running time (times for the immediate value-adding activities) and nonproductive time. The machine running times are determined mainly technologically and can therefore relatively simple mathematical calculation method for using different processing methods (turning, milling, drilling, welding, etc.) can be determined. Nonproductive time are composed of many small percentages of time for individual manipulation. MTM (Method Time Measurement) has already many years ago trying to break them down into individual handling activities and assign a value for each of these activities. The same applies to systems of predetermined times (SVZ). Some companies have created scheduled times from time recording and from schedule time catalogs.

Some companies attract the target times of operations currently performed by detecting the start and end time, and thus calculate the used time. The problem with this form of time determination on the one hand that it is not necessarily the same process steps have to be included—Pick e.g. tool—and then the individual performance (keyword performance level) is not involved.

The boundaries of a technical plan time calculations are required therefor effort. The development of methods known as MTM, SVZ, different calculation method in conjunction with a manufacturing family education (keyword shape key by Opitz), but also the use of existing CAD data and their transfer to CAP system contribute to the improvement of the plan term quality. For more complex structures can be determined by a multiple influencing variables (MER) rapid and sufficiently accurate planning times.

5.2 Socio-Technical Solutions

Technical solutions alone have the disadvantage that the man should be disregarded. But this does not influence the leadership or the person in itself and not its environment are included in the considerations. The practitioner knows but how leadership affects the led and its environment. The question arises therefore as follows: Can be found a system that takes into account the complete capture of all processes the personal influences?

Learning Control ERP-Systems

Operational performance processes also in custom manufacturing usually largely constant process steps (process elements). The production of the individual parts and assemblies can in fact be summarized in so-called manufacturing families; and for these processes are similar. These process steps can be defined similar to the time elements in MTM or systems of predetermined times once.

Operating data is now installed in many manufacturing operations. It is, however, coupled through the workshop order to the work plan. In addition, there are few detectable time elements, which have nothing to do with a workshop order.

However covers all process steps both in content as well as the time required for it, so can be used in a learning system after a sufficient amount of data a "true flow" are defined, which then can be placed further planning is based.

Overcome Limitations of a Self-learning System

The boundaries of a learning process design system lie in the definition of the required for the individual process steps times. Although the detection time is generally not a problem; the problem is that no acquisition system can tell which performance level the task was executed. For the PDM system the recorded time is the fact.

Performance levels differ within a person of his current disposition, and especially from person to person due to different abilities and different drives. It therefore needs not only the collection of quantitative data and the qualitative detection, i.e., performance standards for data. This can be done for example by the production manager (master). Because these individuals, however, cannot follow all the steps of all persons and even then estimate the respective level of performance must be content with the periodic acquisition of sufficient level of performance data for each employee. Again, an error occurs or inaccuracy; However, these are sufficiently accurate and therefore sufficient.

6   Summary

The quality of the detailed planning is determined on the one hand from the "correct" sequence and the other hand of the "right" planned times. The impact of poor data quality includes decreased productivity and poorer delivery reliability.

A solution to these shortcomings is partly in determining proper planning times with the aid of suitable systems—add-in or add-on solutions, including stand-alone possible—and to recognize recurring process steps on the other hand in learning ERP systems that are capable of and this presented in a holistic process.

Ultimately, the quality and usefulness of an ERP system is not showing in the planning accuracy, but in the compliance of planning and implementation. One-minute planning simulates a spurious accuracy, if the differences in reality reach a factor of 10 to even 100 of the planning unit.

Part II
Business Process Models

Potential Benefits of Using Social Software in ERP-Based Business Process Management

Lars Brehm and Rainer Schmidt

Abstract Today, design and improvement of ERP-based business processes are important tasks, requiring quick responses to changed requirements. Furthermore, as many as possible stakeholders should be involved in order to create innovative solutions. Social software has received a lot of attention, because of its capability to unearth new potentials for innovation and collaboration. In this paper we analyze, how social software can support the design and improvement of business processes in the ERP life cycle—with a focus on later phases. We also examine, which mechanisms of social software are most beneficial in which phase of the ERP life cycle. Future research can investigate the usage of social software based on the identified areas in more detail.

1 Introduction

The design of business processes gains management attention just during the initial implementation of the ERP system or in transformational phases, like mergers and acquisitions, carve-outs or business model changes. In the remaining time the business processes should be performed according to the defined design. The continuous improvement of business processes "coded" in the ERP system occurs often only on a reactive basis and is not managed as a priority. Nevertheless, users of the ERP system often spot areas for improvements in their daily execution of business processes, but are reluctant to pass their ideas on. The procedures for participation in business process improvements might be too complex, the change processes too restrictive or too unclear.

L. Brehm (✉) · R. Schmidt
Munich University of Applied Sciences, Munich, Germany
e-mail: Lars.Brehm@hm.edu

R. Schmidt
e-mail: Rainer.Schmidt@hm.edu

© Springer International Publishing Switzerland 2016
F. Piazolo and M. Felderer (eds.), *Multidimensional Views on Enterprise Information Systems*, Lecture Notes in Information Systems and Organisation 12, DOI 10.1007/978-3-319-27043-2_6

Identifying means for establishing a proactive, more bottom-up organized improvement of business processes in the context of ERP-systems would be rather beneficial. At the same time, Social software [1] often called Web 2.0 has received a lot of attention, because of its capability to unearth new potentials for innovation and collaboration.

Therefore, in this paper, we analyze the following research question: How can social software support the design and improvement of business processes in the ERP life cycle—with a focus on later phases? As benefits of the support of social software in the ERP-based Business Process Management (BPM) we see increased productivity, higher output with same costs or same output with less costs, as well as, higher flexibility for future changes in a business process by increased simpli-fication in the process design and/or the corresponding ERP system configuration. The conclusions in this paper are drawn from the extensive experience of the authors in the industry applying ERP-based BPM resp. the academic field of BPM and social software as well as discussions with the colleagues in the field.

The paper proceeds as follows: First, the requirements of business process management in an ERP-context are analyzed. Then social software is introduced and potential effects on business process management in general are identified. After this, the related work is described. Then the application of social software in the ERP life cycle is investigated. Further sections cover limitations and future research. Finally, a conclusion is given.

2 Business Process Management in the ERP-Life Cycle

The activities of Business process management differ substantially across the dif-ferent phases of the life cycle of ERP systems in enterprises. Before the BPM activities are discussed in more details the often cited model by [2] will be pre-sented to explain the different phases of the ERP-life cycle.

2.1 ERP-Life Cycle Phases

Markus and Tanis [2, p. 190] separates four phases reaching from the phase "project chartering" to the phase "Onward and upward". Figure 1 provides an overview about the phases.

The "Chartering" phase contains several activities like preparing the business case for the ERP system adoption, the ERP vendor selection, the decision on the project and the set-up of the project organization.

The "Project" phase is the one generally associated with an ERP system, i.e. the implementation of an ERP system in the adopting enterprise until the system and the end users are "up and running". This configuration and rollout are a major

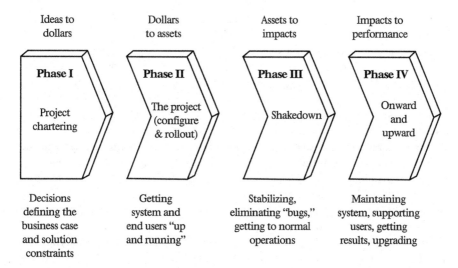

Fig. 1 Phases in ERP life cycle [2, p. 189]

undertaking requiring high efforts and putting the company under high risks. The majority of the research about ERP systems is linked to this phase. Typical activities in this phase are project management, business process reengineering resp. definition, system integration, configuration and adjustment, data conversion, training, testing and change management.

After the going life until "normal operation" has been achieved, this phase is called "Shakedown". The intention of the implementation project is to minimize this phase and the related impact.

The phase "onwards and upwards", also called post-go-live or post-implementation phase, "encompasses the ongoing maintenance and enhancement of the ERP system and relevant business processes. Typical activities include maintaining the system, supporting user, continuous process improvement, and upgrading to new software releases [3, p. 9]".

Additionally, [4, p. 239] proposes an additional phase called "transformation", which is linked to introduction of new business models or major changes in customer structure. Similar effects on the ERP system can be experienced with mergers and acquisitions or carve-outs. For a further discussion on the different phases see also [5].

2.2 Typical BPM Activities in the Phases

The activities in the ERP life cycle are associated with activities from the Business Process Management lifecycle [6]. A business process management system (BPMS)

[7] is a software system that supports the management of business processes. It consists of one or several integrated tools for handling the business process lifecycle. Most business process lifecycles contain the following phases. During the design phase the business process, a model of the business process using approaches such as the Business Process Modeling Notation BPMN [8] or ARIS [9]. Using the formalized process model an implementation is done. Two basic approaches exist. The use of process engines originates from the Workflow Management Coalition (WfMC) reference model [10]. In this approach, the business process model is interpreted, and process instances are created by the process engine. Sometimes, the business process model is transformed into a more execution friendly representation. A notable example is the transformation of the Business Processes Execution Language into BPEL [11]. The second approach is the creation of a materialized process representation that is used for building process instances. The approach can be implemented using composite applications. Composite applications are sets of connected and specialized software components [12]. Sometimes the deployment of the business process is done in a separate phase. After deployment, the business process is in the operation phase. During the operation phase, process instances are created. They represent concrete business transactions such as selling goods. Data representing the execution of the business process instances is collected for later analysis. In the optimization phase, the data logged during the operation phase is analyzed in order to find possible improvements. The operation and optimization phase may overlap. That means, the analysis of logging data may already start during the operation phase.

The implementation and usage of an ERP system fall clearly into the second approach. The definition in [13] describes this as "hard-coded processes". These hard-coded business processes are based on processes alternatives predefined by the vendor as well as the adaptation during the "project phase" with configuration and adjustments by the implementing company and involved third party partners like implementation consultants.

Typical BPM activities in the ERP life cycle phases are: In the "Chartering" phase mainly lists of the relevant processes and high-level process maps are developed or utilized for the ERP vendor selection and project set-up.

During the "Project" phase substantial efforts are utilized to either perform a business process reengineering (BPR) in combination with the ERP system adoption or to analyze, describe, model and (partially) improve resp. adjust the existing processes in order to be able to implement these within the ERP system. In some cases, the documentation and modeling of the processes are performed using a model notation language and supported by a BPM system for managing the documentation and the models. However, often just regular word processing, spreadsheets or presentation/visualization software without a specific model notation language is used.

The aim in the "Shakedown" phase is to shorten this phase as much as possible, so typical BPM activities are "bug-fixing" to the earlier defined processes with a parallel adjustment of the process documentation, which not always also occur.

In the phase "onwards and upwards" the benefits from the new system should be realized. This phase lasts up to several decades (with maybe some transformational phases in between). The benefits are realized by performing the business processes according to the defined design. In this phase incidents, like wrong postings or software errors occur which hinders the successful execution of a business process. These incidents need to be corrected. Companies often utilize the ITIL framework for providing the required support to the business users. Besides errors fixing, there is also the need for smaller or larger process changes resp. adjustments, which might be required due to legal changes, new customers, products or process variants. Requests for change is also part of the ITIL framework, but is often linked to administrative burden. This is one reason for the fact that business users of the ERP system often spot areas for improvements in their daily execution of business processes, but are reluctant to pass on their ideas. Additionally, the corresponding update of the process descriptions and models are often not consistently performed. So in a nutshell, the continuous improvement of business processes "coded" in the ERP system occurs often only on a reactive basis and is not managed as a priority.

In the "Transformation" phase, which is linked to disruptive business events, substantial business process changes are often required. These changes are typically quite time critical and therefore involvement of business users are limited as well as the continuous update of process documentation and models.

3 Using Social Software in Business Process Management

In [1] three issues are identified that hamper the broad use of business process management. The model-reality divide is the loss of synchronization between the business process model and business process implementation. Because many stakeholders are not involved properly into the process design and evolution, they ignore the formal process definition as soon as possible. The lack of information fusioning is caused by the imposed definition of terms. The terms used in process models are not developed collaboratively. Instead, the different usages of terms in different parts of an organization are not dissolved. Furthermore, a lack of organizational integration creates a threshold for information exchange causing a loss innovative potential in business process management.

Social Software [1] is considered as an important means to overcome information-pass-on-barriers and foster process innovation. Social software provides four mechanisms: social production [14], weak ties [15], value-co-creation and egalitarian decision processes [16]. Social production inverses the top-down planning of changes and replaces it with a bottom-up approach. Thus, the areas for business process improvement are not primarily identified by top management but initiated by the users. Social software also leverages weak ties for spotting individuals owning important knowledge. Value-co-creation replaces the tayloristic organization of business process reengineering by a cooperative approach. This allows integrating contributions of users hitherto ignored. Egalitarian decision processes replace expert-based decisions and leverage the wisdom of the crowd.

Social Software is related to a number of other approaches Social media combines social production and weak ties. Social networks establish weak ties [17] and allow collective decisions. The uses of social software within enterprises is called Enterprise 2.0 [18] When social software is used in a business context, this is called social business.

In the following, the effects of social software on business process management in ERP-contexts shall be discussed.

3.1   Social Production

Social production [14] abstains from the tayloristic top-down planning. Instead, the stakeholders decide on their own, whether they contribute. Thus, not a manager decides about production and its management, but the stakeholders. Social production is based on the idea, that the creation of innovation artifacts can be more successful by planning and organizing production collaboratively in a bottom up manner. In this way, social production breaks with classical concepts such as taylorism [19] that plan and organize production in a top-down manner. Before social software, it was very difficult to implement social production because the collaborative planning and organization tasks could not be handled properly.

In [1] social production is decomposed into a number of sub-ordinated concepts: community defined taxonomies, optimistic access policies, continuous information fusioning and aggregation and a quickly rotating improvement cycle.

The use of social production has far-reaching consequences on all phases of BPM lifecycle. Before, the design of business process had been strongly expert-driven. Experts in BPM such as external management consultants were hired to design business processes. However, this approach was criticized due to the following reasons. First, the knowledge and opinions of many stakeholders were not used in this way. The lack of involvement of many stakeholders implied, that it was not possible to convince the stakeholders to adopt the business processes designed by the experts. Often, shortly after the end of the business process project, the old processes were re-established.

Applying social production to BPM means that all artifacts are created with the involvement of as many stakeholders as possible. E.g. using social software, the business process model is created by the collaborative effort of all stakeholders, i.e. the stakeholders themselves are empowered to design the process.

Social production can be applied to other artifacts as well, e.g., the definition of performance indicators can be done collaboratively. In this way, it is possible to define a set of performance indicators that is much more tailored to the needs of the organization. Furthermore, the equilibrium between the need for data and the effort to collect the data can be meet more precisely.

3.2 Collective Decisions

Collective decisions are created by combining independently made decisions of individuals. Examples of collective decisions are votings but also prediction markets [20]. By integrating a huge number of opinions, collective decisions [21] are capable to reduce errors in a statistical manner. Collective decisions provide statistically better results than experts [16]. There may be some experts delivering better results. However, it is not possible to identify the experts that will do so in the future.

The use of collective decisions changes business process management significantly. Instead of following the orders of a superior manager or expert, a large group of individuals has to be involved in the decision procedure. This may need preparatory steps and may last longer than the simple transmission of an order. Collective decisions may not deliver a valid result on the first attempt. Instead, repeated voting may be necessary to get a decision. It is even possible, that no decisions are made.

3.3 Weak Ties

Weak Ties [15] are relations between persons not implied by their organizational affiliation. Weak ties enable the sharing of competencies and experiences in organizations across departmental boundaries. Social software fosters the creation of weak ties by the possibility to establish relations asynchronously and without the need to be in the same places. Furthermore, social software enables the individual to create weak ties deliberately. Before social software, weak ties were created by incident, such as during waiting in the queue of the employees' restaurant. The collaboration following the initiation of weak ties does not necessarily have to happen in software. Capturing weak ties is a supplement to organizational modeling that is contained in many business process modeling tools such as ARIS [9]. These may capture the hierarchical relationships of persons and their role in processes. However, they do not capture contacts created in social networks, competencies etc.

The use of weak ties in the BPM lifecycle changes the dichotomist organization model of traditional BPM. Integrating weak ties, a person is no longer either involved or not. Instead, weak ties of different types may exist. In this way, it is possible to integrate experts for a certain kind of process tasks distributed to different organizational units. Evaluating the weak ties between them helps to solve problems more thoroughly.

3.4   *Value Co-creation*

Value co-creation [22] overcomes the strict separation of the producer and the consumer of goods and services. The consumer of goods and services participates actively in the design and creation of goods and services by providing ideas, suggestion, criticism etc. In this way value co-creation breaks with Taylorism [19] and Fordism [23].

Value co-creation influences business process management in the way that the formerly strictly separated roles of producer and consumer of business process models, e.g. expert and user, are dissolved. Instead, the business user is enabled to provide contributions to the design of the business process. By this means, the creative capabilities of the business process participants can be fully exploited.

4   Related Work

In [24] the positive effects of weak ties, social production and collective decisions to social software and business process management are described in detail. E.g. Social software helps to overcome the model-reality-divide and avoid the loss of innovations. Social software also surmounts the information-pass-on threshold and enables information fusion using a number of mechanisms. Participation of users is eased and change processes are facilitated. Possible changes are made participants for all stakeholders. Information fusion is enabled by a user-defined ontology and the egalitarian inclusion of all stakeholders. In [25] it is shown, how weak ties, social production and collective decisions provide the prerequisites for agile business process management. Collective decisions and weak ties foster the organizational integration of all stakeholders. The semantic integration is provided by social production. The responsiveness of business process management is significantly increased by social production either. In [1] it is shown, that by applying weak ties, collective decisions, social production and value co-creation a number of issues in present business process management can be solved.

5   Applying Social Software to ERP Life Cycle Phases

Applying the principles of social software to conventional BPM, a number of consequences arise as previously discussed in [24, 25]. First, the definitions of business processes (build time) are not done by experts but with the involvement of all stakeholders. Then the participants of the business process (at the run time) are not limited to execute well-defined rules that are implemented in business process models; this allows the creation of weak ties. Third, decisions formerly made by individuals are replaced by collective decisions. In summary, social software allows BPM (at the build and the run time) to stop using waterfall approaches in business process modeling and development. They also liberate us from the use of silo-driven approaches both for business process development and for business process execution. To overcome many of the described shortcomings in the business process management in the ERP life cycle we expect that the usage of social software is beneficial in the following described areas.

5.1 Project Chartering

Project chartering, includes several activities like preparing the business case for the ERP system adoption, the ERP vendor selection, the decision on the project and the set-up of the project organization.

The definition of the business case as well as high level process maps is a complex take that should consider the input of many different stakeholders. Therefore, social production would be very helpful for defining the business case. Project chartering also contains a number of decision tasks that can be supported by collective decision mechanisms of social software. The set-up of the project organization should not only consider hierarchical considerations but also competency-based ones such as represented in weak-ties.

5.2 Project Configuration and Rollout

The "Project" phase embraces the implementation of an ERP system until the system and the end users are operational. Social software could be used to supplement the standard project organization and tools in order to collect additional information about the status, the progress and possible issues during implementation. Also collective decision mechanisms may be helpful to tackle complex problems during implementation. In this phase the use of social software is of course useful to analyze, describe, model, improve or adjust the business processes by utilizing social production and collective decision-making.

5.3 Shakedown

After the going life until "normal operation" has been achieved, this phase is called "Shakedown". The intention of the implementation project is to minimize this phase and the related impact. Social software may be helpful to identify quickly and prioritize hot spots of process execution issues.

5.4   Onward and Upward

This phase covers the post-go-live or post-implementation phase. During this phase, maintenance of the system, supporting user, continuous process improvement, and upgrading to new software releases is performed [3, p. 9].

To handle user requests, events, incident etc. it may be helpful to apply processes and concepts known from ITIL [26]. Consequently, these processes can be supported by social software as described above.

For the phase "onwards and upwards" one major aim is to utilize the knowledge and expertise of the business users, which have to perform their daily tasks with the support of the ERP system. To reduce the burden to run through a formal ITIL request or communicate with some kind of super user an easy participation in social production and collective decisions like rating, voting, tagging or commenting on process improvement potentials would be useful. This functionality should be directly accessible within an ERP transaction (i.e. one-click functionality). By seeing other users' social content weak ties within the enterprise can be detected by the users and be used to address issues and questions linked more indirectly with the hard-coded processes like interpretation of standard operating procedures for certain business processes.

A second aim is to reduce the model-reality-divide, which increases normally in this phase. A starting point is an easy link between the ERP system transactions and the process documentation and models. For capturing the business users' knowledge about the "real" process execution functionalities like in Wikis, which enables easy (text) changes as well as tracking and comparison of the adjustments, should be available for the process documentation and the models.

A third aim is to increase the mutual understanding of the cross-department, cross-country, cross-division interaction in the business processes. Missing or wrong information in one step of the process may lead to major issues in a "far away" downstream step of the process. The social content associated with the process can help to identify the relevant business users, create direct communication and mutual understanding.

5.5   Transformation

The phase transformation is similar to the project configuration and rollout, but requires quicker execution. Therefore, the same social BPM activities as in the project phase can be utilized.

Table 1 Usage of social software in ERP lifecycle phases

	Social production	Collective decisions	Weak ties	Value co-creation
Project chartering	x	x	x	
Project configuration and rollout	x	x		
Shakedown		x		
Onward and upward	x	x	x	x
Transformation	x	x		

5.6 Link to Mechanisms of Social Software

During the ERP life cycle, there are numerous areas for the potentially beneficial use of social software in the ERP-based BPM as shown in the previous sections. To summarize, how this use of social software link back to the mechanisms of social software, the Table 1 provides an overview.

6 Limitations

The proposed usage of social software in the ERP-based BPM needs to be further analyzed regarding the usage in companies—as described in the following chapter. For the above shown application of social software we assumed companies of larger size with several decentralized departments and locations, likely in several countries. For smaller companies the application of social software might be different.

7 Topics for Future Research

As a next step for researcher, which are investigating the social software usage in ERP-based BPM, we suggest to analyze the here presented areas of potential usage with the provided latest software functionality of the ERP software vendors or 3rd providers. This includes also special add-on software components of the software vendors (e.g. SAP StreamWork or SAP Jam). Additionally, the analysis of specific social software usage of ERP using companies, which might be mesh ups of software components and services of several vendors and/or even open source solutions in the proposed areas, is an interesting research area.

Future research will try to leverage social content for identifying relevant patterns and identify improvement potentials in combination with "classical" process mining [27] that analyzes process execution logs. A further challenge to be addressed by future research is the issue, which objects should the created social content be linked to—ERP system transactions, process model activities, ITIL request or other documentation objects. This is for example important for correct filtering for the users to get just "relevant" information in their news stream. Furthermore, compliance and security concerns are a topic for research because the social content generated by users across the company and maybe involve third parties (like application maintenance outsourcing service providers).

8 Conclusion

Social Software can provide substantial benefits to the different phases of business process management in the ERP life cycle as described in this article. This applies especially to the "project" phase and the "onward and upward" phase. In the "onward and upward" phase social BPM activities and social software provide an extra benefit for the enterprise by overcoming the information-pass-on-barrier and fostering process innovation while management attention to business process improvement is reduced.

Additionally, social business process management has also the potential to reduce the mismatch of a companies' business process models with the in reality performed processes—the model-reality-divide.

References

1. Schmidt, R., Nurcan, S.: BPM and social software. In: Ardagna, D., Mecella, M., Yang, J., Aalst, W., Mylopoulos, J., Rosemann, M., Shaw, M.J., Szyperski, C. (eds.) Business Process Management Workshops, pp. 649–658. Springer, Berlin (2009)
2. Markus, M.L., Tanis, C.: The enterprise systems experience-from adoption to success. In: Framing the Domains of IT Research: Glimpsing the Future through the Past, vol. 173, pp. 207–173 (2000)
3. Koh, C., Soh, C., Markus, M.L.: A process theory approach to analyzing ERP implementation and impacts: the case of Revel Asia. J. Inf. Technol. Cases Appl. **2**, 4–23 (2000)
4. Ross, J.W., Vitale, M.R.: The ERP revolution: surviving versus thriving. Inf. Syst. Front. **2**, 233–241 (2000)
5. Shaul, L., Tauber, D.: Critical success factors in enterprise resource planning systems: review of the last decade. ACM Comput. Surv. CSUR. **45**, 55 (2013)
6. Weske, M.: Business Process Management: Concepts, Languages, Architectures. Springer, Berlin (2007)
7. Reijers, H.A.: Implementing BPM systems: the role of process orientation. Bus. Process Manag. J. **12**, 389–409 (2006)
8. Silver, B.: BPMN Method and Style: A Levels-Based Methodology for BPM Process Modeling and Improvement Using BPMN 2.0. Cody-Cassidy Press, Aptos (2009)
9. Scheer, A.W.: ARIS-Business Process Modeling. Springer, Berlin (2000)
10. Fischer, L., Coalition, W.M.: Workflow Handbook 2003: Published in Association with the Workflow Management Coalition (wfmc). Future Strategies Inc., Brampton (2003)

11. Iyengar, A., Jessani, V., Chilanti, M.: WebSphere Business Integration Primer: Process Server, BPEL, SCA, and SOA. IBM Press, Boston (2007)
12. Schmidt, R.: Component-based systems, composite applications and workflow-management. In: Proceedings Workshop Foundations of Component-Based Systems, pp. 206–214. Zürich (1996)
13. Rosemann, M.: Proposals for future BPM research directions. In: Ouyang, C. and Jung, J.-Y. (eds.) Proceedings of the 2nd Asia Pacific Business Process Management Conference. Springer International Publishing, Cham (2014)
14. Benkler, Y.: The Wealth of Networks : How Social Production Transforms Markets and Freedom. Yale University Press, New Haven (2006)
15. Granovetter, M.: The strength of weak ties. Am. J. Sociol. **78**, 1360–1380 (1973)
16. Surowiecki, J.: The Wisdom of Crowds: Why the Many Are Smarter Than the Few and How Collective Wisdom Shapes Business, Economies, Societies and Nations. Anchor (2005)
17. Brambilla, M.: Application and simplification of BPM techniques for personal process management. In: Rosa, M.L., Soffer, P. (eds.) Business Process Management Workshops, pp. 227–233. Springer, Berlin (2013)
18. Andrew, P.: McAfee: Enterprise 2.0: the dawn of emergent collaboration. MIT Sloan Manag. Rev. **47**, 21–28 (2006)
19. Guest, R.H., Aitken, H.G.J.: Taylorism at watertown arsenal: scientific management in action 1908–1915. Technol. Cult. **2**, 191 (1961)
20. Dye, R.: The promise of prediction markets: a roundtable. McKinsey Q. **2**, 82 (2008)
21. Tapscott, D., Williams, A.D.: Wikinomics: How Mass Collaboration Changes Everything. Portfolio (2006)
22. Andreu, L., Sánchez, I., Mele, C.: Value co-creation among retailers and consumers: new insights into the furniture market. J. Retail. Consum. Serv. **17**, 241–250 (2010)
23. Shiomi, H., Wada, K.: Fordism Transformed: The Development of Production Methods in the Automobile Industry. Oxford University Press, Oxford (1995)
24. Erol, S., Granitzer, M., Happ, S., Jantunen, S., Jennings, B., Johannesson, P., Koschmider, A., Nurcan, S., Rossi, D., Schmidt, R.: Combining BPM and social software: contradiction or chance? J. Softw. Maint. Evol. Res. Pract. **22**, 449–476 (2010)
25. Bruno, G., Dengler, F., Jennings, B., Khalaf, R., Nurcan, S., Prilla, M., Sarini, M., Schmidt, R., Silva, R.: Key challenges for enabling agile BPM with social software. J. Softw. Maint. Evol. Res. Pract. **23**, 297–326 (2011)
26. Office, S.: The Official Introduction to the ITIL 3 Service Lifecycle: Office of Government Commerce. The Stationery Office Ltd, London (2007)
27. Van der Aalst, W., Adriansyah, A., de Medeiros, A.K.A., Arcieri, F., Baier, T., Blickle, T., Bose, J.C., van den Brand, P., Brandtjen, R., Buijs, J.: Process Mining Manifesto, pp. 169–194. Business Process Management Workshops (2012)

Creating Event Logs from Heterogeneous, Unstructured Business Data

Sebastian Pospiech, Robert Mertens, Sven Mielke,
Michael Städler and Patrick Söhlke

Abstract Efficient processes give companies the edge required to prevail in global competition. Processes can have a high impact on important factors like product and service quality as well as overall economic efficiency. Hence process improvement plays an increasingly important role in many companies. The first step in process improvement and analysis is understanding the process. While a number of process analysis tools are available, these tools can only analyze processes for which log data (e.g. generated by BPM systems) exists. This paper introduces a tool that allows users to collect and structure traces from undocumented processes like workarounds or improvised processes in order to generate log files. The tool supports query specific ad-hoc exchange of ontologies in order to extract information from unstructured documents containing process traces as well as data extraction components for common databases. It thus bridges the gap between process traces in unstructured, heterogenous documents and process analysis software.

Keywords Process · Mining · Business intelligence · Event log · Transformation · Unstructured data

S. Pospiech (✉)
Cologne Intelligence GmbH, Decision Design, Cologne, Germany
e-mail: sebastian@s-pospiech.de

R. Mertens · S. Mielke · M. Städler
Department of Computer Science, University of Applied Sciences Weserbergland,
Hameln, Germany
e-mail: mertens@hsw-hameln.de

S. Mielke
e-mail: mielke@hsw-hameln.de

M. Städler
e-mail: staedler@hsw-hameln.de

P. Söhlke
Next Vision GmbH, Hessisch Oldendorf, Germany
e-mail: ps@nextvision.info

F. Piazolo and M. Felderer (eds.), *Multidimensional Views on Enterprise Information Systems*, Lecture Notes in Information Systems and Organisation 12,
DOI 10.1007/978-3-319-27043-2_7

1   Introduction

In many companies, some processes like workarounds or adaptations to unexpected events do exist without knowledge of the management. They have not been planned and are not documented. Employees do execute certain tasks intuitively as they think it is correct. Often they stick to a certain order and always fulfill a set of tasks in the same manner. They even might have found a very efficient way of execution. However, since there is no documentation, it is almost impossible to define key performance indicators. Hence it is neither possible to measure the efficiency nor to improve such a hidden process. In order to do so, the process with all its facets must be discovered and documented, best in a standardized process model like an EPC. In a highly digitized company, it might be possible to discover such a process by analyzing the data stored in the company's databases, file storages or mail servers. If there is data that is produced by a certain task of process and then used by the next task of that process, the data could serve as a trace to reproduce the processes steps and their connection. In literature there are hardly any methods which are able to fulfill operations which figure out data sets that can describe a whole process. Various approaches range from analyzing transaction logs [1] to building event based data warehouses [2]. While the first type of approaches are simple to implement but are limited to data being stored in one heterogeneous system, more complex approaches are often too difficult to implement, since they need a highly customized solution. One idea is to use ETL-tools like they are used in classical BI in order to receive data from a database that belongs to a process. This data can then be used by the ETL task to receive data from another database. Such a job would represent a process consisting of two tasks which produce data in the particular database. However, ETL tools are designed for huge data sets. They often lack the abilities to make investigations on single data rows and do only work well on structured data like databases. Our approach describes a similar way to discover processes but with the difference that it is designed to investigate a single process execution's trace by simply searching for and analyzing the data it created and used. In a second step, our software provides methods to expand the specific queries in a way that other executions of the process are found and checked for conformance automatically. The final output of our software is an XML-document containing information about the investigated process executions, extended by semantic information describing the process. It can be shown that this structure is functionally equivalent to an event log as it is used by Process Discovery algorithms.

The remainder of the paper is organized as follows: In the next section we discuss related work. Then we will show the limitations of an ETL-based approach and introduce our software and how it works. We will proof the equality of our softwares output compared to an event log and will demonstrate how to transform that output into a classic event log that can be read by Process Discovery algorithms. This step of transformation is important since it connects a multi-source data analysis of both structured and unstructured data as it is done with our software to classic Process Discovery as it is used in process mining. The paper will conclude with the discussions of the system's role in process analysis.

2 User Story

Imagine Mr. Miller, a business consultant hired by a manufacturing company that has problems with their complaint handling at a specific problem. In order to find out what is going wrong, Mr. Miller has to know what the process of handling customer complaints looks like. Since there is no documentation and no one is aware of a real process but is simply doing his or her job to the best of knowledge, Mr. Miller has to discover the process that probably is behind the complaint handling.

He starts questioning the members of the hotline team. Those note down complaints in the CRM system of the company and link it with the particular customer. Mr Miller can proof that by querying the CRM database and looking for complaints that he takes as an example. For each of these complaints, a serial number of the broken product is attached. He decides to use that serial numbers and looks into the database of the goods receiving department, to check if the broken product has been send back to the company. Thus, the serial number serves as a business key and links the data from one source to another.

Mr. Miller now has reconstructed two steps of the customer complaint handling process: Registering the complaint and receiving and inventory the broken product. This way he can reconstruct the whole process step by step using questionnaires and example data. When he is finished he might want to test if all complaints follow the same process. So he has to reconstruct all the steps for several executions of the process, starting with the entries in the CRM database. He might also want to verify steps of the process that generate unstructured data. A step to inform the customer for example could produce a letter that is stored on the file system of the company. Unstructured data is usually quite more challenging. For efficiently searching in unstructured data it might be necessary not only to search for a certain word but also to look out for synonyms or hyponyms in a certain context. Especially when verifying the reconstructed process with other executions, it might be unsatisfying to always look out manually for corresponding unstructured data.

3 Related Work

Our work is settled in the field of Process Mining that is a part of Business Process Management. One task of Process Mining, Process Discovery, deals with the creation of Process Models for describing and documenting business processes. Creating Process Models can either be performed manually or by using Process

Discovery algorithms [1, 3–7]. These algorithms take event logs as an input and process them to create the model. PROM is an Open Source collection of Process Mining tools that provides various Process Discovery algorithms. Our work focuses on generating event logs that can be loaded into and processed by the PROM software [8].

In this paper we address the problem of creating the event log to be used by a certain discovery algorithm. Usually this log data is being gained directly or indirectly from digital information systems that are used by an agent who performs an undiscovered process [9]. Since business companies often have heterogeneous structures, especially those which have grown very fast or through corporate merges, it is difficult to extract this data. It might be distributed over various databases or simply be stored in unstructured formats on file- or mail-servers. One idea is to use log-files that are originally created for debugging and maintenance purposes: In [6] the logs of a subversion system are used to create an event log describing the software development process which a development team uses to implement their software. A second approach is simply to use the features of a workflow management system to gain the log [10]. A third idea is to use an event-data warehouse. Such a warehouse is structured like a classic warehouse used for Business Intelligence, but it tracks event data for example generated through the daily work of a mail-order company with their mail tracking system. Those three approaches are quite good for a certain purpose, but they all do lack in different things. Most approaches described in literature do only work in a homogeneous environment and only with structured data. They are not capable of creating logs that contain data from various systems. Business Processes which affect several databases can't be recognized completely by them.

4 Why not Use ETL?

The usage of ETL tools to track events, by building up an event data warehouse (see [11]) or in smaller environments simply a data mart or csv output does not have the disadvantage of being limited to homogeneous environments. One of the main purpose of ETL is to connect data from various, heterogeneous systems and integrate it into a specified output.

Other than transporting data for Business Intelligence needs, which almost solely derives from structured sources like databases, business processes often generate unstructured data like e-mails or word files. ETL tools are limited to structured data by design. State of the art ETL software like Talend Data Integration or Microsoft SSIS are not even able to read from an unstructured source. So it is hardly possible to find information or a trace of a hidden process in an unstructured document, using ETL.

In order to run Process Discovery on a hidden process, it is necessary to use the data created by that process as validation. If there is a step in the process in which a letter is send to a customer, than there must exist a document for that letter

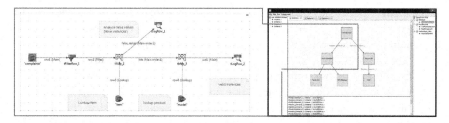

Fig. 1 Comparison between a talend open studio process (*left*) and our Process Explorer

somewhere in the company's network. If it is also possible to find ten additional letters that do all look similar (e.g. having the same keywords like 'claim' or 'return'), then the process has probably been executed ten times and in ten different contexts with that step. In order to use this information in an event log, the analyst trying to discover the process has to analyze the data, try to find such a letter, identify key words and then validate if there exist similar letters to identify other examples of hidden process. For each of those letters, the key information has to be extracted in order to serve as an identification for that instance and to help identify further steps of that process. ETL tools can hardly support users in this task. Their abilities to work with single data sets, visualize and analyze them, are limited and not very comfortable. ETL environments have options to view data just for debugging purposes not to work with the data as a key element to fulfill the task of data extraction.

On the left side of Fig. 1 the ETL tool Talend Open Studio has been used to validate the first two steps of the example use case. The job looks technical, hard to understand for someone who is not a developer. Queries to unstructured components can not be covered and the result of the job shown in the example does not generate an event log but simply prints out the found data. In order to use it for Process Discovery additional transformations which make the job even more complex would be necessary.

5 Process Explorer

Our idea was to design and create a tool that is capable of supporting a consultant or a business analyst in the Process Discovery task as described in the example use case. Our tool is designed similar to classic ETL tools on purpose. The basic idea of retrieving data from various data structures is the same and our target group is familiar with these tools.

On the right side of Fig. 1 a screenshot of the application is shown. The two steps in the red area are semantically equal to the whole Talend ETL process on the left side. The process is being designed in a graph based user interface. Components can be configured to retrieve data from the source systems. A connector is a directed edge that copies data from a source component to a target component. In the example use case, the fist component could access the CRM system and get the serial numbers of the products for which complaints are open. The connector copies these serial numbers to a second component, which then can use the serial number as a business key to look for corresponding information either in another database or on a file server. If there is exactly one corresponding result, this should be the one which was generated in that specific process execution of that complaint. If there is no result or even more than one, this could be a hint on a mistake during the process execution (assuming that the query used to search in the data source is correct). In this case our tool highlights the component in which the query returns an unsatisfying result and the user has to analyze the data for that specific execution.

Because of the need to make detail analysis of certain process executions and its corresponding data, our tool does not behave like an ETL tool and processes many different data sets at a time. It only processes one process execution at a time—each execution in an individual tab. This makes it much easier for the user to analyze how a specific execution behaves and if it is a good representative of the process to be discovered or if it is incorrect. The graphs' structure is not as technical as the one in an ETL tool.

5.1 Searching in Unstructured Documents

Furthermore, our tool can also find information in unstructured documents. In our prototype we provide a component that is capable of handling all basic document types like doc, docx, rtf or odt. Information items stored in unstructured files are neither that easily processable like structured ones, nor is a search in unstructured documents that easy, since natural language is being used.

In order to address the problem of searching information we used a full text search based on elasticsearch and provided different kinds of search methods. First of all, simply searching for a a set of words. Second, searching for a regex pattern and last but not least, searching for a word and all of it's synonyms.

In order to be able to search for a synonym we developed a search engine, that combines the elasticsearch with a triple store to create ad-hoc ontologies for a certain context. We could for example create an ontology describing the semantics of a company's structure. This enables our search component to answer queries like 'Find all documents on the company's file server, which are signed by someone that works in the same department like Mr. Miller'. This feature is important for solving problems when searching in a domain where natural language is used and when trying to find different executions of processes automatically. A business analyst might know because of his examinations that a certain document has been generated by Mr. Miller in the complaint case number 4711, but he does not know if documents of the other complaint cases he wants to use for process re-engineering have also been written by Mr. Miller. Probably they haven't been. Using such an ad-hoc ontology enables a business analyst to search for all members of a business domain without knowledge of all its members. Using predefined ontologies for the English language could help finding documents in which the terminology is not well-defined and may vary from author to author.

6 Connection to Process Discovery

In literature [9, 12], the field of Process Discovery finishes with the creation of a process model. The graph designed in our application so far is not a standardized process model like an EPC or a petri-net. It is rather a trace of the process which has been uncovered by the data (the data is a footprint in that metaphor). What our tool does is actually a step before Process Discovery as being illustrated in Fig. 2. It takes the trace of a process, adds semantic information like a description of the activity and creates an event log as an output, which can serve as an input for a Process Discovery algorithm.

The proof that the graph designed by our tool is compatible to an event log has been introduced in detail in our recent work, see citation number [13]. What the user actually does is creating an event log that is simply designed as a graph and the generalization to all executions. Therefore one basic element of our tool is to convert an event log into a format that is compatible with the PROM framework in order to apply it on a Process Discovery algorithm. The export feature simply iterates through the graph and creates a csv output. For each process execution stored in the graph an ordered list is being generated. Each row in this list represents one event, with the name of the activity, an optional description and an optional

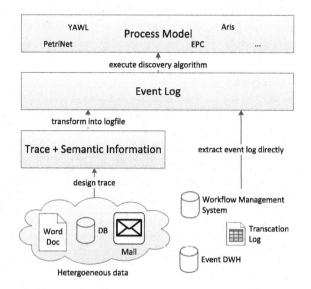

Fig. 2 Process Discovery using our approach (*left*) verses the classic approach

Fig. 3 Sample process
designed using the Process
Explorer

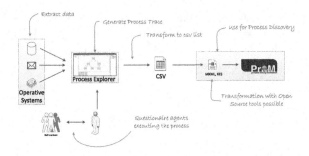

timestamp. The whole workflow of reengineering a process using Process
Discovery (e.g. using Nitro and PROM) and our Process Explorer to create a
process trace representing an event log, can be seen in Fig. 3: A business analyst
uses our tool while talking to the people executing the process to create a trace out
of the data provided by operative systems. He exports the trace into a csv list, which
then can be used by state of the art process mining/Process Discovery software.

7 Conclusion and Outlook

In this paper we introduced a software to be used as a tool supporting process
reengineering by using heterogeneous business data. We have shown that the tool
plays a role in Process Mining and its output can serve as input for Process
Discovery algorithms. In a follow up project the implemented prototype has to be
improved and tested using more advanced ontologies for querying unstructured
documents in a complex business environment. Beside domain specific ontologies
based on company specific structures, ontologies used to improve querying natural
languages like synonym registers could be integrated and used.

References

1. Cook, J.E., Wolf, A.L.: Discovering models of software processes from event-based data.
   ACM Trans. Softw. Eng. Methodol. **7**(3), 215–249. ISSN:1049-331X (1998)
2. Schiefer, J., et al.: Event data warehousing for complex event processing. In: Loucopoulos, P.,
   Cavarero, J.L. (eds.) IEEE, RCIS, pp. 203–212 (2010)
3. van der Aalst, W., van Hee, K.M.: Workow Management: Models, Methods, and Systems.
   Cooperative Information Systems. MIT Press, Cambridge (2004)
4. Agrawal, R., Srikant, R.: Mining sequential patterns. In: Proceedings Data Engineering 95,
   ICDE '95. IEEE Computer Society, Washington, DC, USA, pp. 3–14 (1995)
5. Das, S., Mozer, M.: A unified gradient-descent/clustering architecture for finite state machine
   induction. In: Cowan, J.D., Tesauro, G., Alspector, J. (eds.) Morgan Kaufmann, NIPS, pp. 19–26
   (2003) ISBN:1-55860-322-0

6. Duan, B., Shen, B.: Software process discovery using link analysis. In: IEEE 3rd International Conference on Communication Software and Networks (ICCSN), pp. 60–63 (2011)
7. Werf, J.M., et al.: Process discovery using integer linear programming. In: Proceedings of Petri Nets 08, pp. 368–387. Springer, Heidelberg
8. van Dongen, B.F., et al.: The prom framework: a new era in process mining tool support. In: Proceedings of Petri Nets 05, pp. 444–454. Springer, Miami (2005)
9. van der Aalst, W.M.P.: Process Mining: Discovery, Conformance and Enhancement of Business Processes, 1st edn. Springer, New York (2011). ISBN:3642193447, 9783642193446
10. van der Aalst, W., Weijters, T., Maruster, L.: Workow mining: discovering process models from event logs. IEEE Trans. Knowl. Data Eng. **16**(9), 1128–1142. ISSN:1041-4347 (2004)
11. Casati, F., et al.: A generic solution for warehousing business process data. In: Proceedings of Very Large Data Bases 07. Vienna, Austria: VLDB Endowment, pp. 1128–1137 (2007)
12. van der Aalst, W.M.P., et al.: Process mining manifesto. In: Business Process Management Workshops '11, pp. 169–194 (2011)
13. Pospiech, S., et al.: Exploration and analysis of undocumented processes using heterogeneous and unstructured business data. In: Proceedings of IEEE ICSC 2014, pp. 191–198 (2014)

Knowledge-intensive Business Processes—A Case Study for Disease Management in Farming

Dagmar Auer, Stefan Nadschläger and Josef Küng

Abstract Knowledge-intensive business processes (KIBPs) are strongly connected with knowledge work (KW). Thus, the definition of KW determines the relevant area of KIBPs. KW characteristics such as rather unstructured processes, user-driven, relying on knowledge, need for flexibility, adaptability, creativity and autonomy of knowledge workers are also associated with KIBPs. However, several authors argue based on their empirical findings that KW often also involves pre-defined, repetitive tasks besides a lot of creative work. Furthermore, latest trends put more emphasis on the practice of knowing. Based on our understanding of KW, we study a farming business process, which is not regarded as a typical KW domain. However, when looking at the details, many KIBP characteristics can be identified. Based on a use case dealing with disease management, particularly plant protection, in farming, we evaluate our understanding of KIBPs and thus, prepare the basis for the requirements definition concerning supporting models and methods with respect to adequate IT support.

Keywords Knowledge-intensive business processes · Knowledge work · Knowledge management · Knowledge processing · Farming process

D. Auer (✉) · S. Nadschläger · J. Küng
Institute for Application Oriented Knowledge Processing (FAW),
Johannes Kepler University Linz (JKU), Altenbergerstr. 69, 4040 Linz, Austria
e-mail: dauer@faw.jku.at

S. Nadschläger
e-mail: snadschlaeger@faw.jku.at

J. Küng
e-mail: jkueng@faw.jku.at

© Springer International Publishing Switzerland 2016   95
F. Piazolo and M. Felderer (eds.), *Multidimensional Views on Enterprise
Information Systems*, Lecture Notes in Information Systems and Organisation 12,
DOI 10.1007/978-3-319-27043-2_8

1   Introduction

Knowledge work (KW), defined by Peter F. Drucker in 1959 [1] to distinguish this kind of work from manual work, has been considered as elitist within the working area for years. There has been a heavy increase in KW during the past decades [1, 2]. Still, no common understanding of the term KW has been developed so far. Today, the focus of KW seems to shift towards knowledge in (or at) work [3] and the practice of knowing [4].

Business process management (BPM), with its focus on standardizing and improving business processes, provides important input for building process-aware information systems (PAIS). The stronger focus on KW, demands these PAIS to support a new kind of processes, so-called knowledge intensive business processes (KIBPs), where knowledge is a key factor.

Within the ongoing project CLAFIS (Crop, Livestock and Forests Integrated System for Intelligent Automation) [5], we are dealing with knowledge processing and knowledge management in the context of business processes in sustainable production in farms and forests. Farming is not the traditional domain of knowledge work, but still the question arises, if business processes in farms today are potential KIBPs. As the answer to this question has deep impact on the supporting IT system, we study a key use case in farming, the disease management process, in particular plant protection, concerning important characteristics of KIBPs. The results presented here, also include considerations concerning the implementation of a suitable process-aware information system (PAIS) with explicit support for knowledge management.

In the following section we give a brief overview of the current state of the art concerning relevant concepts such as BPM, knowledge management (KM), KW and KIBPs. The use case disease management with focus on plant protection is described in Sect 3. Section 4 provides a set of characteristics to determine if it can be regarded as KIBP and the results of our case study. Section 5 concludes this paper, by also taking considerations concerning the design of a supporting IT system into account.

2   Related Work

In the following, we will highlight some of the most important aspects within the context of knowledge intensive business processes (KIBPs), such as business process management (BPM), knowledge work (KW), and knowledge management (KM) and knowledge processing (KP).

2.1 Business Process Management

BPM has been established in the tradition of workflow systems. However, the term business process does not imply a certain level of process structure or predictability. Weske [6] defines business process as "... a set of activities that are performed in coordination in an organizational and technical environment. These activities jointly realize a business goal. Each business process is enacted by a single organization, but it may interact with business processes performed by other organizations". There are no constraints concerning the structure, predictability or coordination of the activities.

However, BPM is often associated with well-structured, activity-centric, highly predictable, thus, predefinable processes with a high number of repetitions, where automation pays off. The activity-centric process execution focuses on routing ("what should be done" [7]) and clearly separates between build-time (models) and run-time (instances).

The rising interest in KW demands more flexibility and adaptability of processes, which requires new or at least extended models and methods for building the supporting process-aware information systems (PAIS). The focus is more on "what can be done" [7], leaving decisions and detailed planning to the user. Extending the traditional activity-centric approach to provide more flexibility is one of the proposed responses in theory and practice. Furthermore, declarative models (rule-based, constraint-based) are used to provide a higher level of flexibility than traditional activity-centric approaches [8, 9]. To reduce the number of potential enactments, Jiménez-Ramírez et al. [10] propose multi-objective optimization of enactment plans, before generating configurable imperative business process models from the constraint-based specifications (in the SDeclare language). However, these approaches are still focusing on the control flow and only slightly touch the data perspective.

A higher level of flexibility is often associated with data-driven activation of process activities, where the key driver for the process is no longer a predefined control flow, but the availability of data. This data-centric view is applied in approaches such as case management [11, 12] or object-aware processes [13].

2.2 Knowledge Management and Knowledge Processing

Research and practice are dealing with KM already for decades, but still neither a common concept of KM nor of knowledge exists.

Even though a common understanding of knowledge lacks, some characteristics seem to be common ground such as the distinction between tacit and explicit knowledge (cp. [14, 15]) or personal, organizational (community), and public knowledge, revealing who knows it. While tacit knowledge is bound to the knowing subject, explicit knowledge can be coded and stored as well as transferred as data.

KM is a multidisciplinary field, with important perspectives from business, cognitive/knowledge science, and process/technology [16]. Many definitions of KM share common elements [16–19] such as: (1) coordinating people, technology, processes and organizational structure; (2) knowledge life cycle: acquiring, creating, sharing, applying knowledge and evaluating the outcome; (3) fostering continuous individual and organizational learning.

The basic aim of KM is an effective and efficient use of knowledge to accomplish advantages for the organization by creating business value [16, 20].

KM is rather human-centric, i.e., people are strongly involved as knowledge carriers, but also in documenting, exchanging, communicating and generating knowledge. Thus, the information used is rather coarse-grained, e.g., documents. To communicate, knowledge needs to be transformed to data and backwards. As humans develop different mental models, it cannot be guaranteed that a knowledge object with person A has the same meaning and impact with person B (cp. [20, 21]). This has also to be considered with IT systems for KM support.

IT systems are strongly increasing in importance for adequate support in KM, e.g., enterprise content management systems (EMS), communication and collaboration, but also for exploiting fine-grained information sources (e.g., structured and semi-structured data) with knowledge-based methods (see KP below). The tools can be grouped into four categories, integrating different KM-related functions within the knowledge life cycle: (1) knowledge access: provide access to explicit knowledge that can be shared and transferred; (2) semantic mapping: information presentation, analysis, and decision making; e.g., ontology tools to organize information and knowledge by groups and schemata; (3) knowledge extraction: support structured queries and replies to help mining text and data by interpreting relations among different elements and documents to achieve structured and more articulated answers; (4) collaboration: enable teams to globally share dedicated spaces for managing, editing and publishing materials, live discussions and interactions, and maintaining a repository of materials associated with every step of the process.

KP has some interference with KM. From an IT point of view KP is mostly understood as an aggregation of representing, exploring, searching and reasoning, but also acquiring, integrating and communicating electronic knowledge artifacts. Depending on the representation (non-structured, semi-structured and structured), a different set of methodologies is applied, e.g., the rule-based approach [22].

Still, much of the available knowledge in organizations is not used. Often too much information is collected in reserve, leading to an information overflow [16]. Furthermore, finding the right artifacts empirically proved to take up to 2 hours a day for knowledge workers [23]. Thus, neither effectiveness nor efficiency demands are currently sufficiently met.

2.3 Knowledge Work and Knowledge in Work

In the following, we discuss the terms *knowledge work* and *knowledge in work*. The term knowledge work has been introduced in 1959 by Peter F. Drucker [1] to distinguish it from manual work. This traditional concept of knowledge work is heavily influenced by the underlying type of work and worker. Thus, technical, scientific, or professional work is typically associated with it. This kind of *work* is widely characterized by knowledge as the main asset to create goods and services. It is goal-oriented, rarely predictable, human-driven, and focusing on complex problem solving and the generation of ideas, often demanding a high level of creativity, autonomy and reliability of the knowledge workers (cp. [4, 23–26]). Knowledge workers are typically professionals, technicians such as engineers, scientists, managers, architects, or lawyers, with a high educational level, who work individually and apply theoretical and analytical knowledge, which they acquired through formal education [26, 27].

Terms such as knowledge respectively knowledgeability in work [3, 28] or the practice of knowing [4] are used to describe the current, more comprehensive understanding in the scientific community. Informal education, communicative knowledge, experience, or using organizational as well as external knowledge are missing in the classical view [4, 29]. Knowledge workers not only consume and produce knowledge, but are continuously learning and teaching, strongly based on tacit knowledge. It not only concerns the personal but also the organizational level. Nonaka [15] characterizes knowledge work as "... a way of behaving, indeed a way of being...". Research on knowledge work is by far not complete, there even seems to be currently a new wave of effort in the community.

2.4 Knowledge-intensive Business Processes

Knowledge is intensively involved with knowledge-intensive business processes (KIBPs). Process participants as well as the process owners are knowledge workers, in some cases they are even the same person.

KIBPs are often characterized to be slightly structured, supporting complex work [24] (e.g., planning, interpretation, judgment), the control flow is driven by user decisions or the availability of certain data (conditions), process instance is evolving during runtime, e.g., by adding new activities. Thus, KIBPs exhibit the characteristics of KW such as human-driven, rarely predictable, support for a high level of creativity and autonomy, including much freedom at runtime to adjust the process to the current needs, etc. (cp. Sect 2.3). Even though adaptability, flexibility, and creativity are typically associated with KIBPs, Marjanovic [30] shows that there are processes which are very-well structured, routine, and knowledge-intensive at the same time. Further, Isik et al. [25] reveal that characteristics such as predictability and eligibility for automation are not suitable to differentiate between KIBPs and non-KIBPs.

Even though KIBPs implicitly rely on knowledge, they are not explicitly integrated with KM. Already 10 to 15 years ago there has been a process-oriented focus within the KM community [31–35], based on the activity-centric paradigm. But, none of these approaches became widely accepted; neither in research nor in practice.

Still, to achieve effectiveness and efficiency in using knowledge, the knowledge base needs to be put into the context of the organization's goals and business processes. Furthermore, process knowledge is deeply embedded in the process itself [18] and knowledge workers typically need specific knowledge to perform process-related tasks rather than determining the sequence of these tasks [25].

Before going into details about relevant characteristics of KIBPs, we describe the use case, which is the basis for our further study.

3   Use Case in Farming

Farming today has nothing in common with the perfect idyll often pushed in commercials. Farming, especially with large agricultural enterprises, is strongly relying on computers for management and production tasks. For instance, farm management information systems (FMIS) or farm tractors equipped with GPS-based precision agricultural technology, allowing for precise automated work in the fields [36] are common.

As farming is a complex set of different business processes, we only deal with a small detail here. In the following, we describe the farming scenario we take as the basis for our further discussion—the disease management process, particularly plant protection. We concentrate on this scenario of how to manage a potential disease with an agricultural estate to study in how far we can talk about knowledge work (KW) and knowledge-intensive business processes (KIBP) and thus, the potential role of IT systems.

3.1   Overview of the Disease Management Scenario

The disease management scenario with focus on plant protection describes how farmers can be supported with managing pest, general risks, and invisible threat. Farmer knowledge from different sources needs to be integrated to provide adequate decision support. This knowledge base should not only be open for an individual farmer, but for a community of farmers and other interest groups. Thus, also the question of security, whom to provide which information, etc. is important. Furthermore, besides access to an integrated information platform and decision support by IT systems, communication and collaboration with external experts (e.g., governmental organizations) and peers (i.e., other farmers, the farmer shares information, experience, and even provides dedicated access to individual farming IT services) need to be regarded. At the core of the plant protection scenario is the Plant Disease Forecast Service (PDFS), a core component that will be prototyped throughout the current project.

Actors involved. The disease management process focusses on the individual farmer, who needs to prevent diseases by choosing the right means (seed, spraying, tillage method, etc.), but also to react to upcoming threats to minimize damage. The farmer is supported by IT services/systems, which can be used to manage farm specific information (e.g., soil quality, plants, seeding date, plants of previous years), but also information from outside such as weather predictions, legal sources, manufacturers, retailers, or other farmers within the community.

Activities. Many activities of a contemporary farmer are supported by IT systems. There are typically many different planning, performing, documenting, monitoring (automated as well as human observations) and evaluation activities, with an increasing amount of IT supported communication and collaboration with other farmers (esp. peers), scouts and external experts. The decision sub process we are studying here is strongly based on different data and information sources, a decision support system, as well as communication and collaboration support. Thus, the business process also contains many service tasks, esp. to extract knowledge from different data and information sources, which the farmer controls by setting parameters in the planning phase or providing additional information sources. Then, the farmer checks the results and decides how to proceed and provides feedback to the system. Collaboration and communication can be part of all of these tasks, too.

Information and knowledge sources. To take decisions, the farmer needs many information and knowledge sources. There are public or community specific sources such as legal and label-specific constraints, regulations that need to be considered as well as private/individual information from the FMIS (farm management information system). Furthermore, advisory services (e.g., weather forecast, weather alert), information services (e.g., market analyses, farm advisory, government, labels, fertilizer and seed providers, machine manufacturers), numerous farm-specific sensors for humidity, rainfall, temperature, or wind and observations on the fields, e.g., after some specific events such as a storm, are used (see Fig. 1). The information is provided in structured, unstructured, or semi-structured data, locally, in a community cloud or on the Web. Furthermore, the data varies from historical data such as planting history to continuous sensor measures.

These sources will be also used by the knowledge service (KS) to extract new insights, perform reasoning, or to provide the users the right documents. Thus, this business process is characterized by the use of different, highly specialized information and knowledge sources to support adequate decisions for plant protection. However, human interpretation not only of the results provided by services (e.g., the risk predication from DSS), but also of the situation on site is needed. The farmer takes observations, documents them in various forms (e.g., notes, pictures,

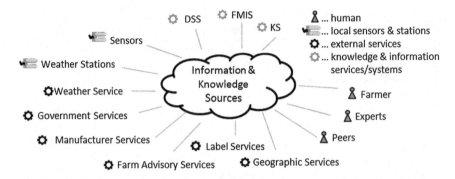

Fig. 1 Information and knowledge resources relevant within the plant protection scenario

voice recording, film, or additional mobile sensors), includes this into the individual decisions and provides feedback for improving future decision processes.

Not only taking decisions, but also monitoring and evaluating the results is important in knowledge generation. This monitoring process captures different kinds of data, information and knowledge (e.g., sensor data, weather data, experiences, interpretation and evaluation of results).

Events. Numerous, different kinds of events may occur during farming business processes. Providing specific support (e.g., advice, best practices) of how to deal with these events should improve the overall outcome. However, this is extremely complex, as farming is very specific to the individual situation (e.g., soil, landscape, humidity, seed, fertilizer, machines, weather, as well as knowledge and experience of the farmer). Furthermore, not all events can be anticipated. Examples for internal events are: problem on the field detected by the farmer, sensor indicates issue, or an engine trouble. External events can concern weather forecast, unexpected legal changes, or current weather conditions.

3.2   Process Model for Plant Protection

The process model in Fig. 2 only describes a high-level view. Thus, this model in BPMN notation does imply an activity-centric approach within our current project. It should only give an impression of the logical ordering of related tasks.

An instance of this business process can be initiated in different ways. Either, the farmer receives some critical observation (by a scout, peer, expert, team member in the fields), manually starts the process (for the current situation or calculates a forecast), or the regular risk calculation by the Decision Support System (DSS) indicates a risk and thus, initiates the farmer's risk handling process. Then the farmer has to check the results, i.e., study the calculated risk, and if anticipated necessary, consult the data and information stores, knowledge resources, communicate with peers, scouts, external experts, etc., ask team members in the fields for

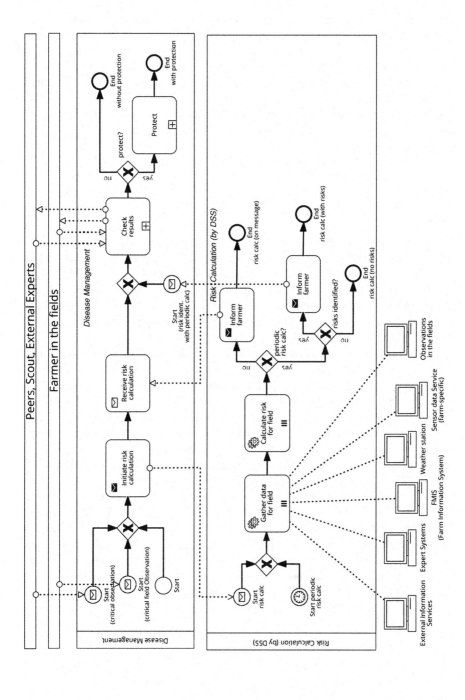

Fig. 2 Overview of the sub process for disease observation and plant protection initiation

additional observations, collaborate with peers, e.g., by jointly studying the results and sources (by offering peers access to selected parts of the individual IT system (s)) and eventually recalculate the risk (not shown in Fig. 2 to keep it simple for this paper) after changing parameters and/or updating input sources. After sufficiently checking the risk assessment, the farmer has to decide, if protection is necessary or not. If necessary, the adequate sub process is initiated to determine and process the appropriate protection, monitor the process (by sensors, observations, etc.) and evaluate the outcome.

Much of the needed data is collected on a regular basis, but there are also additional information sources that are involved on demand, e.g., an inventory control on the fields after a storm.

3.3 Further Considerations

The process described above is only an excerpt of one business process within the complex farming business. It is an idealized model, where prespecified, automated processes (at least to a large extent) seem to be the obvious next step. However, reality is rarely ideal. Thus, when it comes to IT support, not only the idealized process model needs to be regarded, but rather the whole typically iterative planning and disposition process, often turned upside down by internal or external events, which cannot be completely anticipated in advance.

As IT has already entered the world of farming, the amount of available data is heavily rising. Besides different general information services, many sensors are now placed in the fields, on different machines and other equipment throughout the farms. The use of knowledge-based systems will heavily increase, to deal with this large amount of information. Many more aspects can be taken into account by these systems, but still the farmers are the experts within their domain and much of their tacit knowledge has to be integrated into the decisions as well. Thus, there is also the question of how to best use these systems and fit them with the individual ways of work. There is not the one farming business process, as there are numerous facts that influence farming processes, be it differences in soil, weather conditions, availability of seed, fertilizer, machines, but also legal constraints, requirements by the market, certain labels, etc. Still, much knowledge is embedded in the process of performing. Business process models help to abstract, to make this knowledge available for a larger target group. These systems must not be a burden for the farmers, but easing their work concerning time, complexity, exploiting large amounts of available data, communication, and collaboration. Integrating these systems in a work-centric way is an important aspect.

4 Case Study

Our case study is based on the disease management use case with special focus on plant protection described in the previous section. In the further, we will outline the schema for studying the characteristics of KIBPs based on the state of the art described in Sect. 2 and then discuss the assessment of each characteristic in detail.

4.1 Characteristics of KIBPs

The following nine characteristics, shortly described in Table 1, have been identified based on the state of the art described in Sect. 2, to study KIBPs in detail.

In the following section we will present an overview of the assessment results for the disease management process based on the nine characteristics above.

Table 1 Characteristics of KIBPs with short description

Characteristics	Short description
Flexibility	Flexibility concerns anticipated changes of the process instance. These can be considered when starting a process (e.g., variants) or during runtime (e.g., optional tasks). During design time the appropriate model has to be built. Also coarse-grained models allow for more flexibility, but less process support and controlling
Adaptability	Adaptability is about unanticipated runtime changes, evolving process instances, etc.
Activation of task	Describes the typical activation of tasks, e.g., activity-oriented, data-driven, or user-driven
Communication and collaboration	Expresses how important communication and collaboration are within the process, the kind and number of partners involved and to what extent
Creativity	Shows the aspects concerning which creativity is needed, e.g., design time and/or runtime process planning, interaction (see communication and collaboration), or performing the tasks
Autonomy	Describes the extent of autonomy of the actor concerning the process and the concrete tasks to accomplish
Work characteristics concerning knowledge	Combines several aspects such as type of work, use, production, sharing of knowledge, and expertise
Information and knowledge artifacts	Describes the kind of artifacts used, their origin, owner, as well as the transmission and storage media
Context	Identifies the relevant aspects within the process context, their extent, influence, and which actors are concerned

4.2   Discussion of the Characteristics with Our Use Case

In the following, the different aspects for assessing each of the characteristics concerning the disease management process are summarized.

Flexibility. Regarding the farming scenario, there is a well-established high-level process (i.e., coarse-grained), which determines the logical ordering of high-level tasks. There are many situations which can be handled with "standard procedures", which have been adjusted to the specifics of the individual farm. Furthermore, disease management requires a long-term planning of the plant protection products and treatments, as they are typically acquired in autumn the year before, due to lower prices. Thus, the basic conditions can be already predefined to a certain extent, which allows for flexibly choosing the suitable alternative when managing the disease. However, this is not always sufficient and adaptability means are needed.

Adaptability. The disease management process is very complex in detail, as many specifics have to be considered. Not all possible peculiarities (internal and external events, new information and knowledge sources, feedback circles, etc.) can be anticipated—due to financial reasons or because it is simply impossible. Thus, runtime planning and evolving process instances need to be supported. These planning processes take existing artifacts into account and newly defined ones, especially knowledge sources and human tasks. Adaptability is needed with completely new threats, but also when testing changed processes. Information about business processes is important knowledge, which needs to be included into the knowledge base. This is only achievable, if people do not need to rely on work arounds for specific cases.

Activation of task. The process is strongly user-driven, because it is typically the user who decides for the following activity. However, certain preconditions (availability of certain data) can be necessary to allow for activation, indicating a data-centric approach. Furthermore, there are event-driven process initiations, e.g., depending on the outcome of the periodic risk calculation or events affecting running instances, e.g., pest warning needs to be considered immediately.

Communication and collaboration. They are an important part of the scenario. The vision of building a common knowledge base, which integrates general farming knowledge, legal sources, market information, environmental factors, as well as individual, partly private farm-specific information (e.g., FMIS data) and experience, is the basis not only for knowledge services, but also for specific communication and collaboration support. Besides the individual farmers and their teams on the farm, people involved are so-called peers (i.e., farmers who gain access to defined private information for close cooperation), scouts (inform about latest relevant events, changes, etc.) and external experts (are consulted with certain issues).

Creativity. Providing appropriate work support demands for a high level of creativity already when designing the business processes and providing the knowledge sources. However, as already discussed with predefinition, creativity is also needed during runtime—for adequately evolving the business process within the current context, deciding for the right tasks, information and knowledge sources and even developing new processes, tasks and exploiting new information and knowledge.

Autonomy. Assuming that the farmer is the owner or executive of the agricultural enterprise, the farmer has full autonomy concerning decisions and design of the business process (within legal and contractual constrains).

Work characteristics concerning knowledge. The disease management process asks for routine work such as checking certain information and knowledge sources (e.g., the results provided by the DSS), decision taking eventually also based on additional information, but also planning activities. Standard situations are rather routine, but still certain aspects might have changed, demanding for new considerations, leading to slight adaptions up to completely re-planning of the whole process. Thus, also the use of knowledge heavily depends on the situation— standard situation vs. exceptions and single cases. The same is true for knowledge producing, knowledge sharing, and needed expertise.

Information and knowledge artifacts. The information and knowledge artifacts are produced, managed and owned by individuals, communities or the public. They can be structured, semi-structured or unstructured. The better structured, the more predestinated for IT processing, while humans often deal with rather unstructured artifacts. However, specialized methods and software tools to analyze semi- and unstructured information sources to gain knowledge, increase in importance. Information and data sources can be any kind of historic or current artifact, process model, process instance, measure, assessment, or prediction stored in text, tables, film, pictures, audio, etc. Thus, the overall knowledge base contains public up to private knowledge of different kinds, which will be provided to the users through the knowledge service and specific services built thereupon to be best integrated into the working processes.

Context. Regarding the disease management process, many contextual factors are relevant, be it legal, label or market constraints, farm specifics (size, fields, facilities, etc.), situational aspects such as the status of the growth process, seed, field specifics, weather conditions and forecasts.

Table 2 gives a brief overview concerning the assessment of the disease management process.

The case study is not about the highly creative, unstructured, individual process instance, with rare chance to benefit from the knowledge and experience gained for future work. The disease management process contains many predefined parts for standard cases, but needs flexibility and adaptability, a high degree of creativity and autonomy to deal with special cases. Knowledge is a central factor within this rather complex work, with standard cases, but especially the specific ones. Evaluation of existing information and knowledge sources, especially within the context of the process outcomes, is important to continuously improve the knowledge base not only for the individual farmer, but also the community and public (if admitted by the individual farmer).

Table 2 Overview of the assessment of the KIBP characteristics

Characteristics	Assessment
Flexibility	low to high flexibility needs
Adaptability	low to high adaptability needs
Activation of task	user-driven, event-based, data-driven
Communication & collaboration	important
Creativity	standard case: little; specific case: high
Autonomy	high
Work characteristics concerning knowledge	different kinds of work combined, thus different knowledge needs
Information and knowledge artifacts	different sources, owners, structure, kinds, media
Context	complex

Based on these results and further regard to Marjanovic [30] and Isik et al. [25], we consider this process as a sample of a KIBP.

5 Conclusion

With our case study, we revealed that the selected farming process, the disease management, is a knowledge-intensive business process (KIBP). By studying this process, we perceived that this kind of process is heavily increasing in many domains, not to say in nearly all domains, as more and more information and knowledge is available and needs to be considered within the context of the business processes.

The KIBP studied here is characterized by standardized proceedings for standard situations, but evolving for individual ones. Thus, predefinition, flexibility and adaptability need to be integrated to profit from available process knowledge and other information and knowledge artifacts, while being open for dynamically adapting to new or changed situations, when needed. This supports creativity when predefined process models and available information and knowledge sources (knowledge base, decision support systems, etc.) are no longer sufficient, but still provide the basis and context for this work. As knowledge is a key factor of KIBPs, we do not only have to consider the process (model, instance), but especially the involved knowledge—not only its immediate use, but its management and processing.

Designing an IT system, which provides support for KIBPs as identified here, results in a set of complex requirements. Currently, many different approaches are being developed to cope with different aspects and/or forms of KIBPs such as case management [11, 12], object-aware processes [13] or declarative systems [37].

So far, we are right at the starting point of our consideration of how to build an appropriate system providing adequate support for this kind of work. Our next step will be to evaluate existing approaches, not only with respect to flexibility and adaptability, but especially concerning the integration of knowledge, which promises to be crucial for the long-term efficient and effective support of KIBPs.

Acknowledgments The scenario in this paper comes from the EU-PF7-Project Nr. 604659 CLAFIS—Crops Livestock and Forests Integrated System for Intelligent Automation, Processing and Control. The research for this paper is partially supported by this EU project and the State of Upper Austria.

References

1. Drucker, P.F.: Landmarks of Tomorrow: A Report on the New 'Post-Modern' World. Harper & Brothers, New York (1959)
2. OECD: OECD Skills Outlook 2013: First Results from the Survey of Adult Skills. OECD Publishing, Paris (2013)
3. Warhurst, C., Thompson, P.: Mapping knowledge in work: proxies or practices? Work Employ Soc. **20**(4), 787–800 (2006)
4. Rennstam, J., Ashcraft, K.L.: Knowing work: cultivating a practice-based epistemology of knowledge in organization studies. Hum. Relat. **67**(1), 3–25 (2013)
5. CLAFIS: Crop, livestock and forests integrated system for intelligent automation (clafis). http://www.clafis-project.eu/
6. Weske, M.: Business Process Management—Concepts, Languages, Architectures, 2nd edn. Springer, Berlin (2012)
7. van der Aalst, W.M.P., Weske, M., Grünbauer, D.: Case handling: a new paradigm for business process support. Data Knowl. Eng. **53**(2), 129–162 (2005) (Elsevier B.V.)
8. Pesic, M., van der Aalst, W.M.P.: A declarative approach for flexible business processes management. In: Hutchison, D., et al. (eds.) Business Process Management Workshops, LNCS, vol. 4103, pp. 169–180. Springer, Heidelberg (2006)
9. Reichert, M., Weber, B.: Enabling Flexibility in Process-Aware Information Systems: Challenges, Methods, Technologies, 1st edn. Springer, Heidelberg (2012)
10. Jiménez-Ramírez, A., Weber, B., Barba, I., Del Valle, C.: Generating optimized configurable business process models in scenarios subject to uncertainty. Inf. Softw. Technol. **57**, 571–594 (2015) (Elsevier)
11. de Man, H.: Case management: Cordys approach (2009). http://www.bptrends.com/publicationfiles/02-09-ART-BPTrends%20-%20Case%20Management-DeMan%20-final.doc.pdf
12. OMG, Case Management Model and Notation (CMMN): Version 1.0, formal/2014-05-05, http://www.omg.org/spec/CMMN/1.0/
13. Künzle, V., Reichert, M.: Towards object-aware process management systems: Issues, challenges, benefits. In: Halpin, T., Krogstie, J., Nurcan, S., Proper, E., Schmidt, R., Soffer, P., Ukor, R. (eds.) Enterprise, Business-Process and Information Systems Modeling, 10th International Workshop, BPMDS 2009, and 14th International Conference, EMMSAD 2009, held at CAiSE 2009, Amsterdam, The Netherlands, June 8-9, 2009. Proceedings, LNBIP, vol. 29, pp. 197–210. Springer, Heidelberg (2009)
14. Polanyi, M., Sen, A.K.: The tacit dimension. reissue, with a new foreword by Amartya Sen. Univ. of Chicago Press, Chicago Ill. (2009)
15. Nonaka, I.: The knowledge-creating company. reprint of the 1991 article, managing for the long term, best of hbr, nov.-dec. 1991. Harv. Bus. Rev. 162–171 (2007) (Boston)
16. Dalkir, K.: Knowledge Management in Theory and Practice, 1st edn. Elsevier, USA (2005)
17. McElroy, M.W.: The New Knowledge Management: Complexity, Learning, and Sustainable Innovation. Butterworth-Heinemann, Amsterdam (2003)

18. Lehner, F.: Wissensmanagement: Grundlagen, Methoden und technische Unterstützung, 3rd edn. Hanser, München (2009)
19. Liu S., Parmelee, M.: Introduction to knowledge management, http://www.unc.edu/~sunnyliu/inls258/
20. Frey-Luxemburger M.: Wissensmanagement - Grundlagen und praktische Anwendung: Eine Einführung in das IT-gestützte Management der Ressource Wissen. Vieweg+Teubner Verlag, Wiesbaden (2014)
21. Schulz von Thun, F.: Miteinander reden: 1: Störungen und Klärungen. Psychologie der zwischenmenschlichen Kommunikation. Rowohlt, Reinbek bei Hamburg (1985)
22. Bassiliades, N., Governatori, G., Paschke, A. (eds): Rule-Based Reasoning, Programming, and Applications—5th International Symposium, RuleML 2011—Europe, Barcelona, Spain, July 19–21, 2011. Proceedings, LNCS, vol. 6826. Springer (2011)
23. Kelter, J., Rief, S., Bauer, W., Haner, U.E.: Information Work 2009: Office 21-Studie; über die Potenziale von Informations- und Kommunikationstechnologien bei Büro- und Wissensarbeit. Fraunhofer-IRB-Verlag, Stuttgart (2009)
24. Davenport, T.H.: Thinking for a Living: How to get better Performance and Results from Knowledge Workers. Harvard Business School Press, Boston Mass (2005)
25. Isik, Ö., Mertens, W., Van den Bergh, J.: Practices of knowledge intensive process management: quantitative insights. Bus. Process Manag. J. **19**(3), 515–534 (2013)
26. Maier, R.: Knowledge Management Systems—Information and Communication Technologies for Knowledge Management, (3rd edn.). Springer, Berlin (2007)
27. Drucker, P.F.: The new society of organizations. Harv. Bus. Rev. 95–104 (1992)
28. Thompson, P., Warhurst, C., Callaghan, G.: Ignorant theory and knowledgeable workers: Interrogating the connections between knowledge, skills and services. J. Manag. Stud. **38**(7), 923–942 (2001)
29. Ramírez, Y.W., Nembhard, D.A.: Measuring knowledge worker productivity: a taxonomy. J. Intellect. Capital **5**(4), 602–628 (2004)
30. Marjanovic, O.: Towards IS supported coordination in emergent business processes. Bus. Proc. Manag. J. **11**(5), 476–487 (2005)
31. Gronau N., Weber, E.: Management of knowledge intensive business processes. In: Desel, J., Pernici, B., Weske M. (eds.): Business Process Management: Second International Conference, BPM 2004. Potsdam, Germany, June 17–18, 2004. LNCS, vol. 3080, pp. 163–178. Springer (2004)
32. Karagiannis, D., Telesko, R.: The EU-project PROMOTE: A process-oriented approach for knowledge management. In: PAKM 2000, Third International Conference on Practical Aspects of Knowledge Management, Proceedings, ser. CEUR Workshop Proceedings, Reimer, U. Ed., vol. 34. CEUR-WS.org (2000)
33. Papavassiliou, G., Mentzas, G., Abecker, A.: Integrating knowledge modelling in business process management, In: Wrycza, S. (ed): Proceedings of the 10th European Conference on Information Systems, Information Systems and the Future of the Digital Economy, ECIS 2002, Gdansk, Poland, June 6–8 2002, pp. 851–861. http://aisel.aisnet.org/ecis2002/39/
34. Remus, U.: Prozessorientiertes Wissensmanagement: Konzepte und Modellierung. Ph.D. dissertation, Universität Regensburg, Regensburg, 31 May 2002 http://epub.uni-regensburg.de/9925/1/remusdiss.pdf
35. Telesko R., Karagiannis, D.: Process-based knowledge management: experiences with two projects. In: Wrycza, S. (ed): Proceedings of the 10th European Conference on Information Systems, Information Systems and the Future of the Digital Economy, ECIS 2002, Gdansk, Poland, June 6–8, 2002, pp. 964–973. http://aisel.aisnet.org/ecis2002/157/
36. Sorensen, C., Pesonen, L., Fountas, S., Suomi, P., Bochtis, D., Bildsøe, P., Pedersen, S.: A user-centric approach for information modelling in arable farming. Comput. Electron. Agric. **73**(1): 44–55 (2010) (Elsevier)
37. van der Aalst, W.M.P., Pesic, M., Schonenberg, H.: Declarative workflows: balancing between flexibility and support. Comput. Sci.—R&D, **23**(2), 99–113 (2009) (Springer)

Part III
Implementation and Testing Aspects of ERP Systems

Is SAP HANA Useful for Optimization? An Exploration of LP Implementation Alternatives

Karl Kurbel and Dawid Nowak

Abstract While SAP HANA is reported to significantly speed up business information systems that rely on large databases, it is unclear whether HANA has the same power to impact optimization modules. Optimization problems occur both in enterprise resource planning and supply chain management. This paper explores factors influencing the performance of linear optimization programs running inside and outside HANA. Basic simplex implementations in R, SQLScript, JavaScript, and Java are used for comparison. A number of test cases from the Netlib library are employed to evaluate the different approaches and to draw conclusions regarding further research needs.

Keywords Optimization · SAP HANA · Linear programming · SQLScript · R · Javascript · Java

1 Introduction

Many problems encountered in business information systems have been, or can be, formulated as optimization models. In the field of opera-tions research (OR), decades have been spent on developing, refining and implementing optimization methods to solve these problems. Examples include master production scheduling, finite capacity scheduling, sequencing of production orders, vehicle scheduling, and route optimization.

These types of problems occur, for example, in the fields of enterprise resource planning (ERP) and supply chain management (SCM) [1]. Whereas solutions embedded in today's ERP systems are usually based on simple heuristics, "true" optimization algorithms, in a mathematical sense, can increasingly be found in

K. Kurbel (✉) · D. Nowak
Chair of Business Informatics, European University Viadrina Frankfurt (Oder),
Grosse Scharrnstrasse 59, D-15230 Frankfurt (Oder), Germany
e-mail: wi-sek@europa-uni.de

© Springer International Publishing Switzerland 2016
F. Piazolo and M. Felderer (eds.), *Multidimensional Views on Enterprise Information Systems*, Lecture Notes in Information Systems and Organisation 12,
DOI 10.1007/978-3-319-27043-2_9

SCM systems. For example, SAP SCM offers both an optimization approach and a heuristic approach (called SNP heuristic) for one of its core parts, supply network planning (SNP) [2].

With the advent of SAP HANA and SAP's endeavors to base all of their business software on HANA, the question arises if optimization methods can also exploit HANA's power and how in fact this should be done.

Although SAP HANA is often considered a database or a database management system (DBMS), it is actually an "appliance", consisting of both hardware (for hosting and processing in-memory databases) and software—including a DBMS, an IDE (integrated development environment), and application and web servers, among other things [3].

Both SAP and customers stress that HANA is very fast. Compared to conventional relational database management systems, accessing data in HANA databases is by orders of magnitude faster. Plattner reports a performance gain of a factor 100–1000 in comparison to conventional data storage and data retrieval on the application level [4]. This means that data-intensive applications can run extremely fast.

Since most business application systems rely heavily on data, major gains in speed can be expected, and new approaches to known and yet unknown problems may be developed. As Plattner points out, for example, pre-calculated aggregations are not necessary any more, as any type of calculation can be done instantly, on the fly, at an extraordinary speed far beyond that which conventional relational databases would allow [4].

Ideally, the conventional separation of OLAP (online analytical processing) from OLTP (online transaction processing) could become obsolete, because all analytical applications would operate directly on the source data (i.e., on transactional data). This also means that extraction and loading of data into a data warehouse would no longer be required.

In the next section, the motivation for our work dealing with optimization in HANA is described. Section 3 outlines different implementations of a basic simplex algorithms in various languages and settings, while Sect. 4 briefly describes the test cases and the test environment used for numerical tests. Section 5 goes on to discuss the test results, with implementations both inside and outside HANA. Finally, Sect. 6 concludes with a summary of major insights gained and further research needs.

2 Motivation

With the significant improvements provided by HANA in mind, the question arises as to whether HANA does open up comparable opportunities for application areas other than conventional data-based business systems. In this paper, we narrow this question down to optimization methods, in particular to linear programming (LP). This is an area in which research has been proceeding for many decades, and

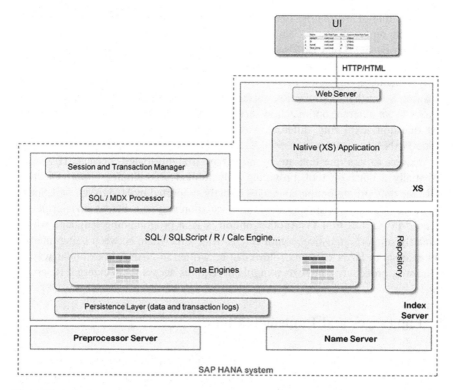

Fig. 1 SAP HANA architecture [8]

powerful optimization algorithms have been implemented. Commercial and open-source toolsets for optimization are available, including Cplex [5], Gurobi [6], and Lingo [7].

The reason why we are nevertheless exploring HANA's capabilities for optimization is as follows. HANA applications are fast when they run *inside* HANA, avoiding (or minimizing) data transfer from the database to an application server over a network. To achieve this goal, HANA includes both an application server and a web server, called XS (extended application services) server, as the outline of HANA's architecture in Fig. 1 shows. This means that in principle, applications can be executed inside HANA, provided that all program code is written in such a way that the XS engine is able to handle it.

In the case of optimization, invoking one of the above mentioned toolsets from a HANA based application program (e.g. a program for supply network planning) would mean that the data making up the optimization model need to be exported in order to be used outside HANA. In other words, HANA's speed would not be exploited. This is only the case if the optimization method is executed inside HANA.

At the time of writing, no implementations of optimization methods for HANA have been reported so far, although this is a critical issue for the success of HANA-based SCM and ERP solutions involving optimization models. Assuming that SAP SCM will also run on HANA in the future, it appears worth checking, firstly, whether optimization inside HANA is feasible and secondly, if this approach performs better than optimization outside HANA (i.e. transferring model data from HANA to an external optimization server). In this paper, we are focussing on the first question, exploring different ways of implementing optimization methods inside HANA.

Answers to this question are by no means straightforward, because HANA is essentially a database tool, providing only limited algorithmic support. Next to SQL, the only programming languages directly supported by HANA are SQLScript and JavaScript. SQLScript is part of the calculation engine, whereas JavaScript can be used in XS (cf. Fig. 1). Another option is R, a programming language which primarily supports statistical computations. R is somewhere between being internal and external to HANA. R procedures can be written in HANA in a similar way to SQLScript procedures, but executing them requires access to an external R server.

3 Languages and Implementations

To be able to judge the suitability of various implementation alternatives, a number of test implementations inside and outside were prepared, carried out, and evaluated. For this purpose, several LP problems were employed and solved with the help of a basic simplex algorithm.

3.1 Implementations Based on HANA

The simplex algorithm was implemented in six different ways, as outlined subsequently, using SQLScript, JavaScript, and R as implementation languages.

SQLScript. Creating procedures in SQLScript is the most "natural" way of programming inside HANA. SQL is the standard language for relational data, with SQLScript providing procedural extensions. SQLScript has algorithmic control structures such as loops and conditional statements. However, it is primarily made for data retrieval and manipulation, not for extensive numeric problem solving. Restrictions apply, for example, to arrays, which can have only one dimension. Two-dimensional arrays are not available.

In our first implementation, we used SQLScript, hoping that HANA's internal mechanisms speeding up conventional applications would also make numeric algorithms faster.

JavaScript. The second HANA native language is JavaScript. Although JavaScript is primarily intended for user-interface tasks, it can also be used to implement algorithmic tasks of substantial complexity. JavaScript provides not only algorithmic control structures but also data structures such as two-dimensional arrays.

R—internal. Creating an R version of the solution appeared to be a reasonable choice for two reasons. Firstly, R is the only other language embedded in HANA. Secondly, due to its main application area—statistical computing—, R comprehensively supports array handling. However, while R procedures are created inside HANA, they are executed on an external R server.

3.2 Implementations Outside HANA

In order to be able to compare execution times in HANA with execution times on a typical computer users would otherwise employ for their every-day problem solving, three versions outside HANA were tested. Admittedly, the notion of a "typical computer" is very vague, but our intention was to gain a basic impression of how HANA-based optimization algorithms perform in comparison to the same algorithms running on conventional computers.

Java. One additional version was developed using a state-of-the-art full-fledged programming language (Java).

R—external-1. The R version mentioned above was implemented once more, outside HANA, to be run from a desktop computer.

R—external-2. As a side effort, we wanted to see how our simple implementation of the simplex method compares to a more professional solution taken from an optimization library supporting R (lpSolve [9]). This solution applies the dual simplex method instead of the primal simplex. In contrast to the previous version, the R procedure invokes a library LP function instead of our self-programmed simplex function.

4 Test Cases and Test Environment

Test cases were taken from the Netlib linear programming library. This is "... a collection of real-life linear programming examples from a variety of sources," [10] available on the Internet. The Netlib library is a common point of reference for authors wishing to test new methods for solving linear optimization problems.

Table 1 briefly summarizes the test problems. In the Netlib LP library, all problems have a name. The first column indicates the library problems we used. The second and third columns specify the numbers of variables and constraints. "Tableau size" is the total number of numerical entries including zeros. For example, AFIRO has 60 columns (32 + 27 + 1, for right-hand side) and 28 rows (27 + 1, for objective function), yielding a product of 60 × 28 = 1,680. The last two columns, "iterations" (i.e. number of simplex iterations until the optimum is found) and "optimum," are just provided as additional information for the reader. The

Table 1 Test cases used for evaluation

Name	Variables	Constraints	Tableau size	Iterations	Optimum
AFIRO	32	27	1,680	15	−464.75
SC50B	48	50	5,049	50	−70.00
SC50A	48	50	5,049	45	−64.58
SC105	103	105	22,154	117	−52.20
SC205	203	205	84,254	359	−52.20
AGG3	302	501	403,608	150	10,312,115.94
AGG2	302	501	403,608	203	−20,239,252.36

"optimum" column is shown here to prove that our implementations actually found the optimum for the respective problem, as reported in the literature.

The hardware configurations used for testing the above mentioned implementations inside and outside HANA have the following characteristics:

HANA server: 32 CPUs (2 GHz), 1 TB RAM
R server: 2 CPUs (2 GHz), 16 GB RAM
Local PC: 4 CPUs (2 GHz) Intel Core Quad, 4 GB RAM

5 Test Results

This section shows and discusses the results of the tests using the various simplex implementations.

5.1 Implementations Inside HANA

As mentioned before, three simplex versions running inside HANA were implemented. The test results (execution times in milliseconds) are shown in Table 2.

Much to our surprise, the *SQLScript* version performed best, although SQLScript is more an extension to SQL than a programming language for implementing computation-intense algorithms. The reason for this good performance is most likely that the data needed to create the simplex tableau are read from a database table. Since the HANA database is integrated with the index server (cf. Fig. 1), SQLScript can access the data very quickly. In addition, it benefits from SQL queries for set processing, and is therefore parallelizable over multiple processors [8].

JavaScript, even though better suited to implementing algorithmic constructs, performed two to three times worse than SQLScript. This is due to the fact that JavaScript runs in XS and needs to access the database form "outside", meaning that data must be transferred between the application server in XS and the database.

Table 2 Test cases used for evaluation of performance on HANA

Name	SQLScript [ms]	JavaScript [ms]	R (on R server) [ms]
AFIRO	35	47	210
SC50B	58	118	633
SC50A	52	102	668
SC105	240	652	4,646
SC205	2,186	6,152	33,945
AGG3	5,587	17,482	102,674
AGG2	6,943	22,548	138,016

The *R* versions performed a good deal worse—in the range of 5–20 times worse than the SQLScript versions. Although R scripts run inside the index server, execution requires access to an external R server. The major factor delaying execution is the need to transfer the tableau data via a network to the R server that finally solves the optimization problem.

5.2 Implementations Outside HANA

With the goal to explore solutions to linear optimization in HANA in mind, it appeared reasonable to make comparisons with external solutions to the same problems outside HANA, on a local computer.

As mentioned before, two versions of the same basic simplex method as used in Sect. 5.1 were tested (Java and R). In contrast to the HANA-based versions, which require a database, these versions read the data directly from a CSV input format into the arrays used in the program code.

The test results (execution times in milliseconds) are shown in Table 3.

Java is probably the best measure to compare a "normal" implementation of an algorithm with any specific implementation format such as on HANA. For the smaller problems (AFIRO to SC105), our SQLScript implementation was faster than the Java version, but for larger problems, Java clearly outperformed SQLScript. We assume that this is a bias resulting from the larger data volume that has to be read from the HANA database table. The Java program, on the other hand, just reads a CSV file to fill the simplex tableau.

The next column shows the execution times of the same basic simplex method implemented in *R*, but now running solely on a local computer. This columns clearly shows the slow-down effect of data transfer to an external R server, which was discussed in Sect. 5.1. Comparing the last column of Table 2 with the "R (basic simplex)" column of Table 3, it becomes evident that the local version is around 2–7 times faster than the server-based version, because no data transfer is required.

All versions discussed so far use the same primal simplex algorithm. Insofar, all results are comparable. However, for "real-life" optimization, much more advanced

Table 3 Test cases used for evaluation of performance on a local PC

Name	Java [ms]	R (basic simplex) [ms]	R (lpSolve) [ms]
AFIRO	42	31	3
SC50B	134	284	4
SC50A	147	318	3
SC105	286	2,344	6
SC205	530	19,579	17
AGG3	945	39,189	34
AGG2	1,296	47,263	35

algorithms would be used. Professional optimization packages usually employ a dual simplex method and specific techniques to handle sparse matrices. Therefore, in addition we also wanted to find out how far the simple primal algorithm is away from a more efficient solution. The test problems were also solved with a dual simplex method used in the *lpSolve* package. The last column of Table 3 shows the results. Obviously, approaches for real-life solutions should employ more advanced techniques than the one used in our tests.

6   Conclusions and Outlook

The work reported in this paper is research-in-progress, and the results obtained so far are inconclusive. We were able to identify certain factors that influence the performance of numeric algorithms—such as the simplex algorithm for linear optimization—and need further investigation.

Surprisingly, the most native language supported by HANA, SQLScript, performed fairly well, although it is not a primary language for numeric problem solving. The performance of R was rather disappointing up to this point. The negative effect of data transfer to an external server seems to overlay all efficient array handling built into R.

The next steps in our research will be to work on the factors that positively or negatively influence the performance. For example, different effects are likely to occur when techniques for sparse matrices are employed. Up to now, all zeros were explicitly stored, as they are part of the simplex tableau. However, in larger optimization problems, where the majority of the coefficients are zero, only non-zero coefficients need to be stored. This will reduce the time needed to read the coefficients from the input table and thus speed up the HANA-based versions.

In particular, the SQLScript version will benefit because most of its performance loss with increasing problem size is due to reading large amounts of data (i.e. zeros). The R version will also benefit from reading fewer data and all the more so from sending smaller amounts of data to the external R server. However, it is doubtful whether this effect can make up for its slow performance compared with SQLScript.

With reference to our initial questions—is optimization inside HANA feasible and is this approach better than optimization outside?—, the answer to the first question is "yes". The second question still needs to be investigated. In further research, we plan to create and test solutions that invoke efficient methods from external optimization packages such as Cplex, and compare these solutions with the solutions developed inside HANA.

For SAP, it might be worth considering to enhance HANA by more efficient native programming languages than SQLScript and R. With appropriate languages, optimization can definitely be provided inside HANA. This approach promises much better performance than solutions outside HANA, because it would strongly benefit from the built-in power of HANA.

References

1. Kurbel, K.: Enterprise Resource Planning and Supply Chain Management. Functions, Business Processes and Software for Manufacturing Companies. Springer, Heidelberg (2013)
2. Hoppe, M.: Sales and Inventory Planning with SAP APO. Galileo Press, Boston (2007)
3. Word, J.: SAP HANA Essentials, 2nd edn. Epistemy Press (2012)
4. Plattner, H.: A common database approach for OLTP and OLAP using an in-memory column database. In: Binning, C., Dageville, B. (eds.) Proceedings of the 2009 ACM SIGMOD International Conference on Management of Data. Providence, RI, June 29–July 2, 2009. ACM, New York (2009)
5. IBM ILOG CPLEX Optimization Studio. http://www-03.ibm.com/software/products/en/ibmilogcpleoptistud/. Accessed 6 Sept 2014
6. Gurobi Optimization. http://www.gurobi.com/en. Accessed 6 Sept 2014
7. LINGO 14.0. Optimization modeling software for linear, nonlinear, and integer programming. http://www.lindo.com/. Accessed 6 Sept 2014
8. SAP SE: SAP HANA Developer Guide—SAP HANA Platform SPS 08, Document Version: 1.1—2014-08-21 (2014). http://help.sap.de/hana/SAP_HANA_Developer_Guide_en.pdf. Accessed 4 Sept 2014
9. Berkelaar, M.: Package 'lpSolve'. Version 5.6.10. http://cran.r-project.org/web/packages/lpSolve/lpSolve.pdf. Accessed 6 Sept 2014
10. Netlib.org: The NETLIB LP test problem set. http://www.netlib.org/lp/data/. Accessed 6 Sept 2014

Fact-Based Declarative Business Rule Modeling for the Static and Dynamic Perspectives in ERP Applications

Peter Bollen

Abstract The fact-based approach (NIAM, ORM, FCO-IM, CogNIAM) provides modeling constructs for the data- and process-oriented perspectives for domain business rules for ERP requirements determination. The event perspective in business rule modeling has been given less emphasis in the fact-based research community. In this paper we will define a number of modeling constructs that allow us to model 'event-perspective' business rule semantics in a declarative way that builds on the existing fact-based modeling constructs for business rules in the data and process perspectives.

1 Introduction

In most, if not all ERP projects there is a need for capturing the initial user requirements (business rules). In this article we will focus on the business rule modeling constructs in the fact-based approach for the the *behaviour-oriented perspective* or *event perspective.* The definition of business rules in the literature ranges from: 'business rules are defined as statements about how the business is done...' [1, p. 147] to: 'business rules specify action on the occurrence of particular business events.' [2, p. 701].

The fact-based approach contains a small set of very powerful modeling constructs that enable analysts to precisely model the data perspective for an application subject area as fact types (*fact business rules* [3, p. 56]) and population (transition) constraints (*constraint business rules* [3, p. 56]) using a methodology that includes a validation process for the in-between modeling results. Some dialects in the fact-based approach (ORM [4], CogNIAM [5, 6]) have introduced modeling constructs for the process perspectives like derivation rules (*derivation*

P. Bollen (✉)
Department of Organization & Strategy, School of Business Economics, Maastricht University, P.O. Box 616, 6200MD Maastricht, The Netherlands
e-mail: p.bollen@maastrichtuniversity.nl

© Springer International Publishing Switzerland 2016
F. Piazolo and M. Felderer (eds.), *Multidimensional Views on Enterprise Information Systems*, Lecture Notes in Information Systems and Organisation 12, DOI 10.1007/978-3-319-27043-2_10

123

business rules [3, p. 56]) and *exchange rules* [5]. In this article we will define fact-based modeling constructs and methodology for the *behaviour-oriented* or *event* perspective that will enable analysts to better validate the modeling outcome for this perspective.

2 The Information and Process Perspectives in Fact-Based Modeling

2.1 The Insurance Application Subject Area

The running example in this article, is a 'scaled-down' part of an insurance application process of a fictive insurance company INSUR. INSUR provides a large number of insurances for individual clients and businesses. Among these different types of insurance types are *car* and *health* insurance. The insurance application can be described as follows. An individual request for an insurance policy of a specific type is directed at INSUR. Depending upon client's credibility status it is decided to accept or reject the applicant's request. The acceptance criterion is as follows. If the client has at least one order rating in the past that is bad, the application will be rejected.

An excerpt of the list of definitions for the verbs, entity- and value types for the application domain is provided (*definition business rules* [3, p. 56]) in Fig. 1 [7]. Figure 2 shows the content of the fact-based conceptual schema that consists of fact type diagrams, fact type forms, ground facts and the instances of the population state constraints. We note in Fig. 3 how the derivation rule pre-condition references the object types that are specified in the process argument and possibly references the instances of the (ingredient) fact types that must be contained in the application information base. We note that the derivation rule post-condition specifies what the result will be of the execution of the derivation rule, whenever the pre-condition evaluates to true. We note that the *create* operator tells us that the fact instance that will be 'created' has subsequently to be inserted to the application's information base. The created fact will be *added* to the information base when the conceptual information processor (CIP) [8, p. 35] accepts the transaction[1] in terms of information base consistency. If the projected information base after the proposed insert transaction violates the application's conceptual schema (information model) a created fact will **not** be added to the application's information base. The rule-body of the derivation rule contains the explicit derivation logic that 'computes' the value (s) for the 'derived' role for the fact instance(s) that will be created and proposed to the information base.

---

[1]We distinguish *insert, update* and *delete* transaction types on the information base [5]. We will further refer to these transaction types as *exchange rules* [5, 6].

List of definitions for operations management subject: Insurance application	
Insurance Application	a request from an outside actor to the INSUR insurance company requesting to consider issuing an insurance policy
Application Code	a unique signification for an [Insurance Application] that enables us to identify a specific [Insurance Application] within the set of all [Insurance Application]s within the context of the insurance organization INSUR.
Customer	an individual that has or is planning to perform an [Insurance Application]
Customer Code	a unique signification for a [Customer] that enables us to identify a specific [Customer] within the set of all [Customer]s within the context of the INSUR insurance organization.

Fig. 1 Excerpt from list of definitions

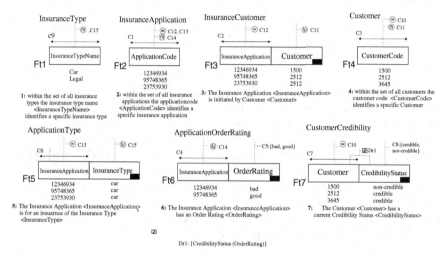

Fig. 2 Fact-based conceptual schema and example information base using CogNIAM graphical conventions

Dr1:	**Derive credibility status <(arg1: customer)>**	
IF	There exists an instance of Ft3	SUCH THAT FT3.customer = 'arg1'
AND	There exists at least one instance of Ft6 (where 'FT6.insuranceapplication' is SUCH THAT there exist an instance of Ft3 SUCH that Ft3.customer =' arg1')	[pre-condition]
THEN	Create an instance of fact type Ft7 SUCH THAT Ft7.customer= 'arg1'	
AND	Ft7.credibilitystatus= DRbody1	[post-condition]
	DRbody1:= IF there exists at least one instance of Ft6 SUCH THAT Ft6.orderrating = 'bad'	
	THEN ' not credible'	
	ELSE 'credible'	
		[rule body]

Fig. 3 Derivation rule DR1 with explicit pre- and post conditions and rule body

The rule-body has a name of itself, implying that the same rule-body can be contained in more than one derivation rule. This allows for declarative derivation rule logic.

3   The Event-Condition-Action (ECA) Modeling
Constructs in Fact-Based Modeling

Although the execution of the derivation rule is constrained by the *pre-conditions* and *post-conditions*, there still remain degrees of freedom with respect to *when* and in *what sequence* these derivation rules or exchange rules can be executed. The *application event description* of a subject area, therefore is needed, to specify **when** the instances of derivation rules from the *conceptual schema* will be executed. These 'rule' executions will be triggered by events. For example the occurrence of an event instance that an *insurance application* is created will 'trigger' the derivation rule: *derive customer credibility*:

```
ON    insurance application is created
THEN  derive customer credibility
```

After the customer has applied for an insurance policy and the customer credibility has been determined, the insurance application will either be accepted or rejected. The event 'insurance application is created' can be considered a 'database event' [9], 'data event' [10, p. 260] or 'an event based on data sources' [11, p. 13] since it coincides with the addition of a fact instance (of fact type Ft2 in Fig. 2) into the information base (or change in the information base state in general). These types of events can be easily 'verbalized' by using the sentence group verbalization template in the CogNIAM information model (see Fig. 2). For example inserting a fact instance of Ft3 in which Ft3.insuranceapplication='12346934' and Ft3.customer='1500' can be verbalized as:

The fact: '**insurance application** with **application code** *12346934* is initiated by **customer** with **customer code** *1500*' is inserted into the information base.

In terms of verbalizing this 'database event' we can potentially distinguish among two 'event object types', namely *customer* and *insurance application*. We can further group the former verbalization of events and qualify them into the *event type*.

Definition 1. An *event type* is a class of events in the application subject area, each of these events can lead to the execution of one or more derivation rules.

In order to make a distinction into fact types and event types we will model the *'role(s)'* in an event type as *event argument(s)*. The object type that plays such a role in an event type in principle is defined in the same way as the object type in the information perspective. In the case of 'external event types' such a specific object type that is defined in an event type, however, does not necessarily have to be defined in the application information model of that subject area. We will now formalize the object types of the event type by structuring these(is) object type(s) into the *event type argument set*. We will derive the set of arguments for the event type by *classifying* and *qualifying* a significant set of verbalizations of event instances, for example:

An insurance **application** with **application code** *257892* is created.
An insurance **application** with **application code** *257893* is created.

This will result in the following event type and its argument set:

Insurance application created (arg1: insurance application[2])

Definition 2. An *event type argument set* of a given event type specifies all object types, instances of which should be supplied at the occurence of an event instance of the event type.

An *event* can start the execution of a derivation rule or exchange rule (in some cases) under (a) condition(s) on the information base. In the population constraints from the application information model we have modeled the 'invariant' business rules that must hold for every information base state. For example the business rule that states that *every insurance application must state the insurance type*. In the pre-condition of the derivation rule(s), the business rules are modeled that specify what ingredient fact instances should be available in order to 'compose' or 'derive' the resulting fact instance(s) in the derivation rule [12, p. 1519]. In the event perspective we will model the business rules that contain the knowledge under what condition (on the application information base) an event of an event type will trigger a specific derivation rule or exchange rule.

Example extension:
In the business subject area for the insurance application it is decided to have the credibility checked not only when an insurance application is created but also on a yearly basis for existing customers.

The new event description for the insurance application example will look as follows:
```
ON E1:  insurance  application  is  created  (arg1:
        insuranceapplication)
THEN    derive customer credibility (arg1:customer)
ON E2:  new day (arg1: date, arg2: month)
IF C1:  (E2.arg1 = '1' AND E2.arg2 = 'january')
THEN    FOR ALL customers in Ft3.customer
        derive customer credibility (arg1:customer)
```

The verbalization of these event dynamics is as follows:

E1: If the **insurance type** for the **insurance application** is created then the **credibility** of its **customer** must be derived
E2: If a **new day** begins and that day is *January 1st* then the **credibility** of every **customer** must be derived

---

[2]It is sufficient to only denote the object type in the event argument. The accompanying naming convention for the object type is captured in the fact-based information diagram (see Fig. 2 for this example).

We can see that there exist two different types of events that can lead to the execution of (different) instances of the same derivation rule (in this case the derivation rule *derive customer credibility*). In this example events of two **different** event types will lead to the triggering of the **same** derivation rule. When an event instance of the first event type (E1) (e.g. An insurance **application** with **application code** *257892* is created) occurs the derivation rule will be 'triggered' unconditionally. When an instance of a 'pure event source' [1, p. 13] occurs, e.g. the event type E2 (e.g. A new day with a **date** having **datecode** *15* and a **month** with **monthname** *January*) occurs a guard condition exists that will only allow those event instances to trigger whose argument values fulfill the guard condition. The latter model of event execution can be considered a general case of an event-condition-action or ECA rule [13, p. 16, 14, pp. 139–140] [15, p. 137].

A *guard condition* acts as a *constraint* for the execution of a derivation rule or exchange rule that is 'triggered' by a specific event.

```
ON    E1:insurance application created(arg1:insuranceapplication)
IF    C2: Ft5.insurancetype= 'car'(where Ft5.insuranceapplication
                                              ='El.arg1')
THEN DR1: derive customer credibility (arg1:customer)
```

The verbalization of the above ECA rule is as follows:

If the **insurance type** for the **insurance application** is created and the **insurance application** is a *car* insurance then the **credibility** of its **customer** must be determined.

We note that the guard condition type in this example can be instantiated into a *guard condition* on the information base as follows:

Example

Event type *insurance application created (arg1:insuranceapplication)*
Event instance *insurance application created (arg1: '257892')*

Under the condition that the type of insurance is 'car insurance', this event should lead to the execution of the following derivation rule: *derive customer credibility (arg1: customer)*. A different event occurence of the same type is *insurance application created (arg1: "257892")*. Because the type of this insurance application is not a car insurance, the event occurence should **not** lead to the execution of the credibility checking derivation rule(s). In most business application areas it is possible to specify these conditions on a type level: *"If an insurance application is created for a car insurance the customer must have a positive credibility rating."* A condition (or condition instance) of the aforementioned condition type is:

If an **insurance application** *257892* is created then **customer** *064567* must have a *positive* **credibility rating**.

The above example illustrates that the instantiation values for the event type can be used in this case for the instantiation of a condition on the information base:

```
ON E1:insurance application created(arg1='257892')
   IF     C2:Ft5.insurancetype     =     'car'(where     Ft5.
insuranceapplication='257892')
   THEN DR1: derive customer credibility (arg1='064567')
```

Definition 3. A *guard condition* is a proposition on the information base.
Example

$$c_1 : \quad \exists_{f \in EXT(FT1)} [f. <r2> =' Piet']$$

The proposition in the guard condition can contain a reference to one or more instances of the event argument.

3.1   The Impulse Mapper

In many cases the derivation rules are executed under responsibility of different user groups in the same organization or different organizations. We will call the effect of an event occurence into the execution of one derivation rule or exchange rule (eventually under a condition on the information base) an *impulse* (instance). It is this definition of an impulse that allows us to look at an impulse as a specific type of 'business constraint' (see the discussion in [16, pp. 112–113]) and does not have to worry about run-time implementation issues like *code generation* [17], *message sending* [18, p. 132] and *software components* (e.g. *event handler* [19]). Events that do not have the potential to 'trigger' derivation rules or exchange rules are not relevant for the description of the behavioural perspective in a given application subject area [20, p. 3]. We can now classify all impulses that have the same *event type*, the same *derivation rule* or *exchange rule* and the same *condition type* into a set of impulse instances that belong to the same *impulse type*. An impulse type contains an event type, a guard condition type, and a derivation rule or exchange rule.

A construct in the event perspective is now introduced that enables us to derive the instantiation value for the derivation rule- or exchange rule argument in an impulse whenever the values of the *event type argument set* are known. This is the construct of an *impulse mapper* which is a mechanism that encodes the business rules in the subject area that specify *how* a derivation rule or exchange rule is instantiated when an event occurs and the condition on the information base is satisfied.

Definition 4 An *impulse mapper* is a construct that transforms values of event type arguments and fact instances from the application information base into instantiation values for the *argument set(s)* for the derivation rule or exchange rule that will be instantiated in the impulse.

Fig. 4 Impulse type and
impulse mapper

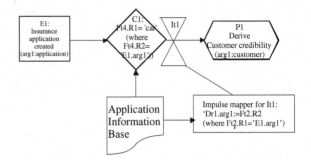

Example:
    Event type   *E1: insurance application created (arg1: insuranceapplication).*
    Derivation rule   *Dr1: determine customer credibility (arg1:customer).*
    Guard Condition type   *C1 : Ft5.insurancetype ='car' (where*
                                          FT5.insuranceapplication='E1.arg1')
    Impulse type   *IT1:=<E1, C1, Dr1>*
    Impulse mapper   *Dr1.arg1:=Ft3.customer (where Ft3.insuranceapplication ='E1.arg1')*

The verbalization of the impulse type (including impulse mapper) in Fig. 4 is as
follows:

> If the **insurance type** for the **insurance application** is created and the **insurance appli-
> cation** is a *car* insurance then the **credibility** of the **customer** <u>who has applied for the</u>
> <u>insurance</u> must be determined.

4   Conclusion

In this paper we have proposed a set of fact-based business rule modeling constructs
for the event perspective in an application subject area. We have thereby explicitly
referenced the application conceptual schema for the models in the data and process
perspectives. The basic modeling construct for the behavioral perspective is the
event (type). The event type interacts with the data perspective in the form of the
impulse-condition, and subsequently it interacts with the process-oriented perspective by referencing the derivation rule(s) or exchange rule(s) that must be
executed whenever the impulse-condition is true. The fact-based application conceptual schema (or information model), the application process base and the
application event description in combination constitute the collection of business
rules for an application subject area. The partial business rule models for these
perspectives, thereby easily map to implementation models, e.g. relational tables,
integrity constraints, stored procedures, methods, database triggers, messages
without sacrificing conceptual clarity.

References

1. Herbst, H., Business rules in systems analysis: a meta-model and repository system. Inf. Syst. **21**(2), 147–166 (1996)
2. Kardasis, P., Loucopoulos, P.: Expressing and organising business rules. Inf. Softw. Technol. **46**, 701–718 (2004)
3. Rai, V.K., Anantaram, C.: Structuring business rules interactions. Electron. Commer. Res. Appl. **3**, 54–73 (2004)
4. Halpin, T., Morgan, T..: Information Modeling and Relational Databases; from Conceptual Analysis to Logical Design, 2nd edn. Morgan-Kaufman, San-Francisco (2008)
5. Nijssen, M., Lemmens, I.: Verbalization for business rules and two flavors of verbalization for fact examples. In: OTM Workshops 2008. Springer, Monterrey (2008)
6. Bollen, P.: Enterprise resource planning requirements process: the need for semantic verification. Lect. Notes Inf. Syst. Organ. **4**, 53–67 (2013)
7. Bollen, P.: Extending the ORM conceptual schema design procedure with the capturing of the domain ontology. In: *EMMSAD '07.*2007. Tapir, Trondheim, Norway
8. Halpin, T.: Information Modeling and Relational Databases; From Conceptual Analysis to Logical Design. Morgan Kaufmann, San Francisco (2001)
9. Rolland, C.: Database dynamics. Data base (spring): pp. 32–43 (1983)
10. Casati, F., Fugini, M., Mirbel, I.: An environment for designing exceptions in workflows. Inf. Syst. **24**(3), 255–273 (1999)
11. Koschel, A., Lockemann, P.C: Distributed events in active database systems: Letting the genie out of the bottle. Data Knowl. Eng. **25**, 11–28 (1998)
12. Bollen, P.: Conceptual process configurations in enterprise knowledge management systems. In: Applied Computing 2006. ACM, Dijon, France
13. Diaz, O., Piattini, M., Caleor, C.: Measuring triggering-interaction complexity on active databases. Inf. Syst. **26**(1), 15–34 (2001)
14. Adaikkalavan, R., Chakravarthy, S.: SnoopIB: interval-based event specification and detection for active databases. Data Knowl. Eng. **59**, 139–165 (2006)
15. Tan, C.W., Goh, A.: Implementing ECA rules in an active database. Knowl.-Based Syst. **12**, 137–144 (1999)
16. Bollen, P.: On the applicability of requirements determination methods. In: Management and Organization. University of Groningen: Groningen. p. 219 (2004)
17. Dietrich, S.W., et al.: Component adaptation for event-based application integration using active rules. J. Syst. Softw. **79**(12), 1725–1734 (2006)
18. Bassiliades, N., Vlahavas, I.: Processing production rules in DEVICE, an active knowledge base system. Data Knowl. Eng. **24**, 117–155 (1997)
19. Pissinou, N., Makki, K., Krishnamurthy, R.: An ECA object service to support active distributed objects. Inf. Sci. **100**, 63–104 (1997)
20. Paton, W., (ed.): Active rules in database systems. In: Gries, D. (ed.) Monographs in Computer Science. Springer, New York (1999)

Towards a Concept for Enterprise Systems Landscape Testing

Johannes Keckeis, Michal Dolezel and Michael Felderer

Abstract In this paper, a concept towards productive enterprise systems testing is presented. Identified challenges, including research gaps derived from literature, are discussed. These challenges and research gaps can initially be confirmed based on results of the herein presented survey analysis. Hence, a concept of an enterprise systems landscape is proposed and combined to the ERP testing stage model.

Keywords Enterprise resource planning · Enterprise systems · Enterprise systems landscape · Testing · ERP testing · Enterprise systems testing · Software testing · Survey · Quality assurance · Software quality

1 Introduction

In today's organizations, ERP systems are an essential and critical part of operational business. Conventional wisdom defines ERP systems as commercial, off-the-shelf (COTS), i.e. packaged software [1, 12]. In contrast to custom-build enterprise software, packaged software is often considered to be thoroughly tested by vendors. However, such a paradigm is problematic at least for two reasons. First, in today's complex and integrated enterprise worlds, full confidence in vendors' testing process may unexpectedly result in eye-opening moments [13]. Second, ERP systems must often be tailored to specific needs of individual customers.

J. Keckeis (✉) · M. Felderer
University of Innsbruck, Innsbruck, Austria
e-mail: johannes.keckeis@uibk.ac.at

M. Felderer
e-mail: michael.felderer@uibk.ac.at

M. Dolezel
University of Economics Prague, Prague, Czech Republic
e-mail: michal.dolezel@vse.cz

© Springer International Publishing Switzerland 2016
F. Piazolo and M. Felderer (eds.), *Multidimensional Views on Enterprise Information Systems*, Lecture Notes in Information Systems and Organisation 12, DOI 10.1007/978-3-319-27043-2_11

In these situations, appropriate testing processes, assuring adequate testing of customized parts, must be established by the customer or by a 3rd party.

Recent software engineering research has emerged the topics and concepts of software ecosystems as an emerging and novel topic [4, 10]. In principle, ERP systems development is an example of activity conducted within the frame of these software ecosystems. Software ecosystem can be defined as "set of [software] businesses functioning as a unit and interacting with a shared market" [10].

But how does the reality of software ecosystems change software testing of enterprise software? In traditional software development models, the majority of testing activities are performed by the software vendor. However, if a system had to be customized for individual needs by a 3rd party, the vendor usually does not warrant correct functional transactions. Some Vendors even discourage customizing practice at source-code level. Thus it can be stated that these ERP customizations "challenge some of the most basic assumptions of software engineering" [3], because development practices substantially differ from standard development approaches when a system is built *from scratch*. This also applies to testing.

Unfortunately, current research literature neither presents adequate empirical evidence how these ERP-related software processes are executed in real organizations, nor provides conceptual guidelines for these challenges. We argue that in the end, when enterprise systems go live, their quality is often poor as testing is done inadequately. This is also a matter of missing systematic approaches and a missing concept for this type of testing. Therefore, our aim in this paper is to provide necessary conceptual background concepts as well as initial results from our survey focused on ERP testing, in order to face issues in this area.

2 Enterprise Systems Engineering

According to SWEBOK's [8] adopted definition of software engineering, the field encompasses "the application of a systematic, disciplined, quantifiable approach to the development, operation, and maintenance of software; that is, the application of engineering to software." This definition points out that all three areas, i.e. software development, operation and maintenance, should be equally presented in the field as its key themes. We however argue that the field is currently predominated mainly by *software development* topics, especially in the context different from typical enterprise software setting. In this paper, we further examine consequences of this fact on the problem area of packaged software testing, especially testing in organizational context and business processes.

In recent two decades, packaged software (COTS software) has gained growing importance in organizations of all sizes due to various reasons, e.g. costs, risks, time-to-market, "best of breed" strategies. *"In fact, the trend for more than a decade has been for midsized and larger organizations to purchase (or lease, often from a service provider) application packages rather than custom develop their own solutions with in-house IS personnel, whenever it is feasible and cost beneficial to do so"* [2].

However, in reality the situation is not as straightforward as presented in IS textbooks like the one referenced above where software is either completely packaged or completely custom-build. In reality, implemented software resides somewhere in between those extremes. For example, packaged ERP systems are often subject to customer-specific modifications due to multiple reasons.

While in the past, "the alternative to reengineering, customizing ERP source code to meet unique organizational needs, ... [was] unacceptable even where possible" [7] for many enterprises, nowadays the situation seems more ambiguous. Many enterprises have already recognized that business process reengineering—forced by implementation of packaged ERP software—is not a universal treatment for their illnesses, and that reasonable amount of customization/tailoring of an ERP package can be a reasonable demand. Thus, ERP customization/tailoring became an important topic for the industry. Dittrich et al. [3] recently performed a survey of ERP *customization practices*. They found three categories of ERP customization activities: (1) simply customizations involving changes in reports, (2) mid-size customization involving an enhancement of existing system functionality, and (3) development of new add-ons in form of so-called *verticals* which represent "independent complementary functionalities with a limited interface to the standard system". In their research activities, they identified testing as one of key cornerstones for successful ERP implementation when customization is involved. Similarly, in another seminal paper related to ERP tailoring [1], several tailoring types were identified.

3   ERP Testing

For some people, (re)-testing of packaged software may seem controversial. "A common perception held by many people is that since a vendor developed the software, much of the testing responsibility is carried by the software vendor. However, people are learning that as they buy and deploy COTS-based systems, the test activities are not necessarily reduced, but shifted to other types of testing not seen on some in-house developed systems" [13]. So, at least in the enterprise systems environment the nature of testing is changing due to customization of COTS and need for their integration. Testing should not be omitted, not even for software already tested by vendors, and Rice argues that new "types" of testing are emerging.

When considering evolving operational context of a software system beyond traditional development activities, *system* life cycle [9] can serve as a tool for conceptualization of respective phases. In software engineering area, SWEBOK understands *software* development life cycle (SDLC) as an integrated set of processes concentrated around software development activities. That above all means to *put a software system into organizational context* in which this software system is going to operate.

Software customization for enterprise systems is mostly done in two ways: Code changes are implemented in isolated parts of the system or they are being "sliced into the standard code". According to Dittrich et al. [3], testing of tailored ERP is very challenging, especially when customization has been done by the second method. In such cases, code changes which were "sliced into the standard code" can jeopardize existing functionality. That in fact implies that customization providers should care also about regression testing of potentially impacted standard functionality. But such complex testing is rarely an option under given circumstances. Furthermore, it would impose the necessity of considering various data and configuration modes. Therefore, reality shows that the scope of testing often "depends on the customer's willingness to pay for the extra effort."

4 Testing in ERP Projects

In this section, we present first results and trends of the state of the art analysis of (end user conducted) testing in ERP projects. Based on that analysis, two aspects in ERP testing are investigated: the system and technical perspective on the one hand as well as the business perspective of ERP testing on the other hand. The setting and methodology of the questionnaire is documented in chapter [5]. The number of responses per question (sample size is max. 97) is provided in the caption of each diagram.

4.1 End User Specific ERP-System Modifications

Figure 1 presents the usage of different system types; 81.44 % of all used systems in our sample are vendor-provided ERP systems and 18.56 % of the used ERP systems are in-house developed systems. In-house developed systems are self-/individual developed ERP systems.

Figure 2 shows different areas of possible modifications and the average across all modifications. Figure 2 additionally differs by whom the modification was implemented. Based on our survey, in total (sum external and internal), on average of over 70 % of all ERP customers employ a modified ERP system. This circumstance is interesting because in total over 80 % of all quoted systems are vendor-provided COTS and only 18.56 % are in-house developed systems (see Fig. 1).

Taking main modifications into account, in total (sum of in-house and externally performed) 88.66 % of the end users modified their systems via customizing and parametrization. Over 80 % modify documents and reports.

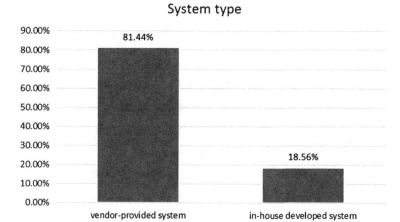

Fig. 1 System type; N = 97

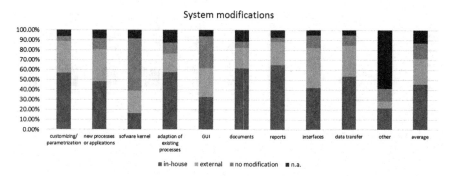

Fig. 2 System modifications; N = 97

Focusing on "software-development-driven" modifications, 80.41 % implemented new processes/applications and 76.29 % adapted existing processes in the used ERP systems. It is also interesting, that over 80 % modified the used ERP systems concerning interfaces to other systems.

Figure 3 shows the three "software-development-driven" reasons, why end users modify ERP systems. 57.73 % modified their ERP system due to missing functionalities. Besides the missing functionalities, 57.73 % of the respondents had to modify the ERP system due to missing or insufficiently implemented interfaces to other systems. Finally, 51.55 % of modifications are based on newly developed requirements which accrued during the implementation phase (see Figs. 4 and 5).

Figure 6 shows the satisfaction with modifications. The satisfaction level differs depending on the modification type. On average, 55.36 % of all end users are either satisfied or very satisfied with their modification. If we focus on the degree of satisfaction it can be seen, that on average 21.24 % are very satisfied and 34.12 %

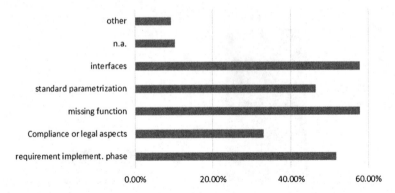

Fig. 3 Reasons for modification; N = 97

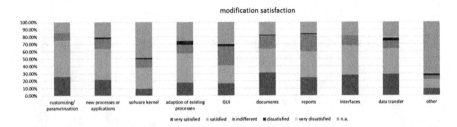

Fig. 4 Modifications satisfaction; N = 97

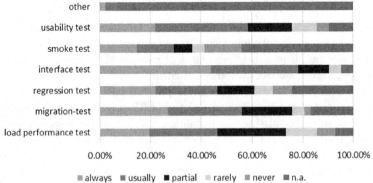

Fig. 5 Test types; N = 41

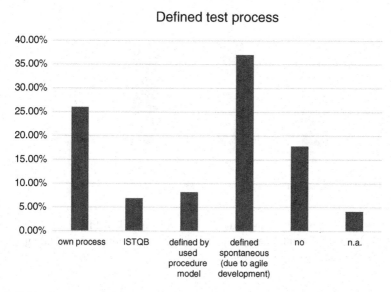

Fig. 6 Defined test process; N = 73

are satisfied with the modifications. Focusing on the satisfaction with "software-development-driven" modifications, it can be concluded that 63.92 % are happy with the development of new processes/applications and 57.73 % are happy with the adaption of existing processes. 68.04 % are "happy" with the modifications on interface level.

4.2 Test Types

In this section, we investigate the used test types. In Fig. 5 the used test types are presented in detail. Interface tests are performed by 78.05 % (sum of always and usually) of all participants. Hence, we conclude that nearly 80 % use and work with a multitude of integrated systems. Migrations tests are conducted by 56.10 %.

4.3 Test Management

In this section, we present the results due to test management. As illustrated in Fig. 6, test processes are used by 78.08 % (sum of mentioned test processes). Nearly 37 % use a spontaneous defined test process due to agile software development. 16.03 % of the participants use self-defined test processes.

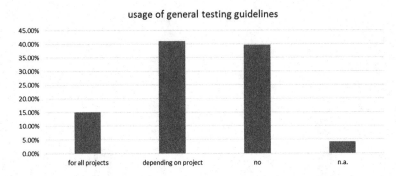

Fig. 7 Usage of general testing guidelines; N = 73

The usage of general testing guidelines is illustrated in Fig. 7. It reveals that 39.73 % do not use guidelines, 41.10 % use testing guidelines depending on the project; and 15.07 % always use guidelines.

4.4 Test Tools

In this section we focus on the usage of test tools in ERP projects. The results are presented in Fig. 8. It can be observed that the usage of test tools is not that common in ERP projects since 54.39 % do not use test tools at all. Only 26.32 % use test tools in some of their projects.

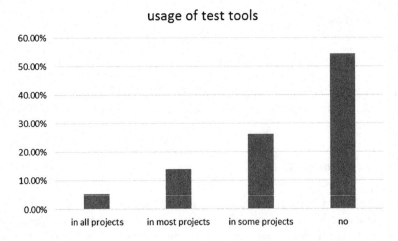

Fig. 8 Test tools; N = 57

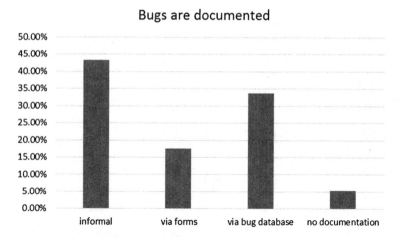

Fig. 9 Bug report; N = 74

4.5 Test Reports

In this section we focus on test reports, the quality of test cases and bug fixing. First, we present the results of how bugs are documented.

94.59 % (sum informal, form based and database documentation) of all identified bugs are documented as pointed out in Fig. 9. This indicates that documentation of the bugs is very important. 43.24 % of all bugs are documented informally, 33.78 % via a bug database and 17.57 % via forms.

The effectiveness of the test cases is illustrated in Fig. 10. 58.11 % evaluate the effectiveness of the used test cases as high (most bugs are identified) and 5.41 % as very high (nearly all bugs are identified). Hence, we can conclude, that the quality of the used test cases seems to be ok. 27.03 % quote that the effectiveness of the used test cases is moderate (some bugs are identified).

The quality of bug fixing seems to be also very high as shown in Fig. 11. 70.27 % quote, that after deployment of the fix, only a few bugs are still present. It is interesting, that 16.21 % (sum of some and fatal bugs and too much fatal bugs) of the bugs are not well corrected.

5 Enterprise Systems Landscape Testing

As shown in Fig. 2, over 80 % modified their ERP systems in order to implement interfaces to other systems. Thus it can be concluded that the majority of end users employ at least one additional software system besides their ERP system. We define these bundles (minimum two) of systems as an enterprise systems landscape. These

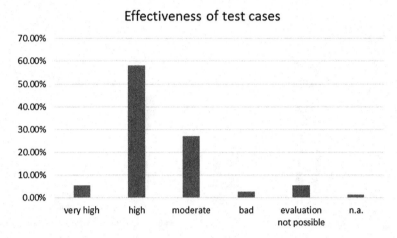

Fig. 10 Effectiveness of test cases; N = 74

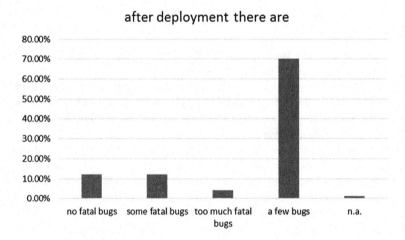

Fig. 11 Bugs after deployment; N = 744

different systems are for example financial accounting, ERP, warehousing, and many more.

Before we present an abstract concept of an enterprise systems landscape, we provide an excursion to three different systems types (see Fig. 12) including a focus in the testing domain.

Excursion

The development of new functionalities and/or code changes are usually not performed in one single system [12] but rather on a multitude of connected systems.

Fig. 12 System types and
software logistic

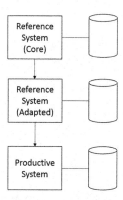

Figure 12 schematically presents three system-types and the flow of software logistics to transport these developments and code changes.

1. Reference System (Core)

A reference system (core system) represents one COTS (packaged software) and is developed, tested, deployed and provided by software-vendors and depicts a core system. There are no organizational specifics (end-user-specific) tailored or customized.

2. Reference System (Adapted)

The adapted reference system represents one COTS and is developed, tested, deployed and provided by software-vendors (often implementation-partners) and depicts a core system. Adapted reference systems are usually extended reference systems (core systems). Such extensions often are:

(1) verticals and/or
(2) branch-specific-modifications and extensions/expansions and/or
(3) new (e.g. vertical and/or branch-specific) functionalities.

There are no organizational specifics (end-user-specifics). We also address such systems as 'reference system'.

3. Productive System

A productive system represents one COTS. We define productive systems as extended reference systems (or adapted). Such extensions often are:

(1) Organizational-specific customizing and parametrization
(2) Organizational-specific modifications
(3) Organizational-specific expansions
(4) Organizational-specific new functionalities.

Productive systems are organizational (customer/end user) specific and contain all organizational extensions. These systems are often linked via interfaces to other

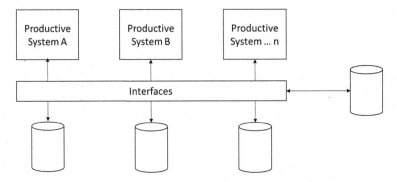

Fig. 13 Enterprise system landscape

software systems, process live data and business processes. Hence, productive systems are operational systems on customer side, to process live data and business processes

Enterprise Systems Landscape Testing

In general, ERP manufacturers, vendors, and implementation partners focus solely on testing their new developments, improvements, and changes within their provided core systems (reference and adapted systems).

End users however, focus on testing productive systems within their individual, customer-specific enterprise systems landscapes. ERP systems are usually the most essential system within an enterprise systems landscape. This bundle of different enterprise systems is usually end-user-specific and the set of systems usually interoperates via interfaces. Figure 13 presents an abstract structure of an enterprise systems landscape.

Based on customer-specific requirements and business processes, relevant customization, adaption/modification, migration, and integration steps are defined for each system.

Thus, it can be concluded that the testing approach of end users is different to the testing approach of vendors, because end users focus on the business perspective and their specific bundle of different systems within an enterprise systems landscape while vendors focus on new functionalities and adaptions based on their software development road map.

This means that the end user test process has to be extended from a single enterprise system to an integrative enterprise systems landscape test process including the end user specific organizational context and the usage of different productive enterprise systems.

This end-user-centric-view distinguishes different project—and/or adjustment types we identified in the literature and as a result of the survey:

- Implementation Project: Implementation of a new enterprise system including integration in the existing/new enterprise systems landscape

- Adaption/Modification Project: Adaption/Modification of new/existing functionalities including integration in the enterprise systems landscape
- Migration Project: Migration to a new enterprise system including integration in the enterprise systems landscape.

6 Conclusion

In this paper, we presented a concept towards enterprise systems landscape testing. In general, the SWEBOK knowledge area seems to omit the context in which testing is performed. For example, the area of systems integration testing is covered by a SWEBOK's statement in following manner. "External interfaces to other applications, utilities, hardware devices, or the operating environments are also usually evaluated at this [i.e. system] level. "Unfortunately, no further guidelines in this direction are provided by SWEBOK and the problem of application landscape (or enterprise systems landscape) testing, i.e. testing "the entirety of all business applications and their relationships in an organization", is unclear although one has several reasons to believe that this type of testing can be considered as a key success factors in the domain of enterprise application integration [cf. 6]. The influence of operational and organizational environment is only briefly discussed in Software Requirements and Software Maintenance in SWEBOK's knowledge areas. So, we can conclude that regarding testing in a unique organizational context (including customization testing of enterprise systems), there is a serious research gap in current SE/IS literature. This gap could potentially be bridged by research, probing into specific issues of testing, in the ERP integration domain. However, testing-specific research seems to be very scarce [11].

Our first analysis of the survey provides an initial confirmation of this research gap. The first results and trends presented in the state of the art analysis exhibit that testing in ERP projects is important to end users because over 88 % of the respondents modified their productive ERP system. Nearly 60 % of the respondents had to modify the ERP system due to interfaces (to integrate the ERP system to other systems). The survey also shows, that nearly 80 % perform interface tests. Thus, we assume that most interfaces are developed customer-specific to integrate their enterprise systems. Over 50 % identify missing functionalities during the implementation process. Therefore one can conclude that identifying requirements ex ante could be improved. Thus, a gap between the business-processes offered by core systems and the customers' business-processes seems to exist. "Software-development-driven" modifications, like implementing or adapting existing functionalities, and the interoperability via interfaces, are the main types and reasons for modification.

A limitation to the validity of the presented results is the fact that the survey has not been fully concluded yet. Therefore, we currently offer a preview of the state of the art analysis based on identified tendencies.

Future research will present a more profound analysis of state of the art of ERP project testing once the data gathering and statistical analysis (including validation of methods is concluded. Hence, we will be able to define the scope of the technical and the business perspective of testing in ERP projects. Furthermore, we will investigate other possible influences on the enterprise system landscape. Thus, we will extend our research approach beside the technical perspective (interfaces) also to the business perspective (business processes). We will also extend the ERP-testing stage model presented in [5] with the concept of testing within enterprise systems landscape.

Acknowledgments This work was partially funded by the research project "QE LaB—Living Models for Open Systems" (FFG 822740), SERES Unit—Sustainable Evaluation and Research in Enterprise Systems and a scholarship grant by the "Aktion Österreich-Tschechien".

References

1. Brehm, L., et al.: Tailoring ERP systems: a spectrum of choices and their implications. In: Proceedings of the 34th Annual Hawaii International Conference on System Sciences, pp. 1–9 (2001)
2. Brown, C.V., et al.: Managing Information Technology. Prentice Hall, Upper Saddle River (2012)
3. Dittrich, Y., et al.: ERP customization as software engineering: knowledge sharing and cooperation. IEEE Softw. **26**(6), 41–47 (2009)
4. Dittrich, Y.: Software engineering beyond the project—sustaining software ecosystems. Inf. Softw. Technol. **56**(11), 1436–1456 (2014)
5. Felderer, M., Keckeis, J.: Design of a questionnaire on testing in ERP projects. Novel Methods and Technologies for Enterprise Information Systems. ERP Future 2013 Conference, Vienna, pp. 109–117 (2014)
6. Gericke, A., Klesse, M.: Success factors of application integration: an exploratory analysis. Commun. AIS **27**(1), 677–694 (2010)
7. Hirt, S.G., Swanson, E.B.: Emergent maintenance of ERP: new roles and relationships. J. Softw. Maint. Evol. Res. Pract. **13**(6), 373–387 (2001)
8. IEEE: Guide to the Software Engineering Body of Knowledge—v3.0 (2014)
9. ISO/IEC/IEEE: ISO/IEC/IEEE 24765:2010. Systems and software engineering—Vocabulary (2010)
10. Jansen, S., et al.: A sense of community: a research agenda for software ecosystems. In: 31st International Conference on Software Engineering—Companion, pp. 187–190 (2009)
11. Kähkönen, T., et al.: What do we know about ERP integration? In: International Conference on Enterprise Information Systems, pp. 51–67 (2013)
12. Ng, C.S.P., Gable, G.G.: Maintaining ERP packaged software—a revelatory case study. J. Inf. Technol. **25**(1), 65–90 (2010)
13. Rice, R.W.: Testing COTS-based applications. http://www.riceconsulting.com/articles/testing-COTS-based-applications.htm

Part IV
Software Usability of ERP Systems

Measuring ERP Usability from the Users' Perspective

Lukas Paa, Felix Piazolo, Kurt Promberger and Johannes Keckeis

Abstract Among several factors, satisfied users have a strong impact on a successful implementation and operation of enterprise resource planning (ERP) systems. The software usability can contribute significantly to reduce the necessary end user trainings and to raise the productivity and satisfaction of users. Despite the awareness of the impact of the usability on the productivity of users there still exists a lack of usability testing concerning ERP systems from software providers and companies as customers. Gathered information of independent evaluations of the usability of ERP systems can support the decision for or against certain providers. This article gives some insight on how to measure usability from the end users' perspective, and also demonstrates first results conducted by a study involving ERP system customers.

Keywords ERP system · Usability testing · Software usability

L. Paa (✉) · F. Piazolo
Andrássy University Budapest, Pollack Mihály Tér 3, Budapest 1088, Hungary
e-mail: lukas.paa@andrassyuni.hu
URL: http://www.andrassyuni.hu

F. Piazolo
e-mail: felix.piazolo@andrassyuni.hu

L. Paa · F. Piazolo · K. Promberger · J. Keckeis
Department of Strategic Management, Marketing and Tourism, University of Innsbruck,
Universitätsstraße 15, 6020 Innsbruck, Austria
e-mail: kurt.promberger@uibk.ac.at
URL: http://www.uibk.ac.at/smt/

J. Keckeis
e-mail: johannes.keckeis@uibk.ac.at

© Springer International Publishing Switzerland 2016   149
F. Piazolo and M. Felderer (eds.), *Multidimensional Views on Enterprise Information Systems*, Lecture Notes in Information Systems and Organisation 12, DOI 10.1007/978-3-319-27043-2_12

1   Introduction

Enterprise resource planning (ERP) systems are known to be complex, extensive to implement and difficult for end users to learn [1]. During the last two decades enterprises, public management institutions and non-profit organizations spent a huge amount of financial and personal resources on the implementation of ERP systems. If the potential advertised by ERP providers really benefits the companies highly depends on the effective use and the satisfaction of end users. That is why lower complexity of the ERP system, simple adaptability of the user interface and customized documentation of the software compose critical success factors [2]. Surprisingly companies rarely observe this aspect which forms a considerable amount of their employee's daily working routine [3]. "Usability is not a luxury but a basic ingredient in software systems: People's productivity and comfort relate directly to the usability of the software they use" [4]. Therefore usability and end user training are highly relevant aspects concerning the actual value an enterprise system is able to create [5]. This study has its focus on the usability of ERP systems and the different approaches to measure it.

1.1   The Term "Software Usability"

Usability describes the quality of interaction between the human and a human-made object. This broad definition also includes software. The quality of interactive software can be described by a vast variety of terms like handling, user friendliness, ease of use and learnability [6]. Software usability describes the quality of the interaction with the software experienced by the user. Technical aspects in this context are only relevant as they have an impact on the use of the software [6]. So instead of investigating the technical quality of the software, usability is concerned with the effect on the working space as well as the impact on users. The software is evaluated concerning the fulfilment of requirements and reliability. ISO defines usability as "The extent to which a product can be used by specified users to achieve specified goals with effectiveness, efficiency, and satisfaction in a specified context of use." DIN EN ISO 9241-11 uses efficiency (Are the deployed resources in relation to the results?), effectiveness (Does the software enable the user to solve his tasks?) and user satisfaction (Is the user satisfied with the results achieved with support of the software?) as criteria to determine the usability of the software [7].

1.2   Benefits of Usability

An estimated amount of 20 % of working time spent on the PC are not productive because of avoidable problems the user experiences [8]. Poorly designed software not only causes financial loss to the company applying the software, but also to providers as they suffer from overcrowded support services and a loss of reputation. In general the benefit of usability composes of three components: raise in productivity, reduction of costs and higher competitiveness [9]. Software providers confirm that the benefits of high usability outweigh the necessary costs to achieve it by far. According to IBM every Euro spent in improvement of usability saves between 10 € and 100 € [10]. This benefit justifies the huge share of the software development budget usually reserved for aspects of better usability which are estimated to rise from 10 % today up to 20 % in the future [9]. The value of software usability, which demands for intense and costly development, which is especially true for ERP-systems, is considerably high.

Higher usability from the customer and user perspective [6]

- increases learnability and thereby reduces training costs
- lowers errors conducted by users
- cuts support costs
- reduces maintenance expenses
- enhances user satisfaction
- raises the overall satisfaction by employees

Higher usability from the provider perspective [6]

- creates new ideas
- results in certainty of success
- enhances predictability
- lowers development costs
- reduces development time
- lowers costs of documentation
- attracts new customers
- increases image and loyalty
- bears advantages in marketing

For both parties, the software vendors and the software customers, an outstanding usability can result in competitive advantages due to a more effective use of the ERP system in operation.

2 Usability Testing

Usability testing defines the process of evaluation if the targeted usability is achieved. Available methods can be categorized in interrogations, observations and experiments as illustrated in Fig. 1. In 2006 researchers at the University of Innsbruck developed a survey to measure the usability of ERP systems from the end users' perspective [6]. Existing measuring methods which are tested on validity and comprehensibility like SUMI (Software Usability Measurement Inventory), SUS (System Usability Scale), ErgoNorm and IsoMetrics were screened by the

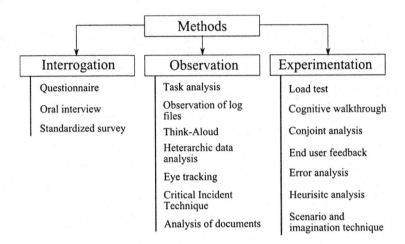

Fig. 1 Categorization of methods to gather data for usability studies

researchers. These will be presented in this paper in order to make the further proceeding transparent.

2.1 Software Usability Measurement Inventory (SUMI)

SUMI is an internationally standardized method to measure the perceived quality of use (user satisfaction) of software [11, 12]. SUMI not only examines the performance but also emotions of users towards the software [13]. The corresponding survey consists of five dimensions, each of which is measured by ten items [13–17]. Considered dimensions are efficiency, affect, helpfulness, control and learnability.

The items are standardized with the option to answer with "agree", "don't know" and "don't agree". Additionally there is a global scale, which consists of 25 of the 50 items, which represents the usability construct most accurately [18].

2.2 System Usability Scale (SUS)

SUS assumes that an overall perception of the software usability is sufficient [19]. It utilizes ten items. Each item gets rated on a five point Likert scale. Following table presents the items used to measure the software usability according to SUS (Table 1).

Table 1 SUS

	SUS items
I	I think that I would like to use this system frequently
II	I found the system unnecessarily complex
III	I thought the system was easy to use
IV	I think that I would need the support of a technical person to be able to use this system
V	I found the various functions in this system were well integrated
VI	I thought there was too much inconsistency in the system
VII	I would imagine that most people would learn to use this system very quickly
VIII	I found the system very cumbersome to use
IX	I felt very confident using the system
X	I needed to learn a lot of things before I could get going with this system

2.3 ErgoNorm

ErgoNorm aims at the detection of shortcomings concerning the usability in order to enhance the quality of the software [20]. The items deployed in the ErgoNorm testing procedure are designed according the DIN EN ISO 9241-10 [21]. The process is divided in two parts: the subjective evaluation by users and a testing procedure conducted by experts [21]. As a result there are 27 selected items, which the user has to rate according to their relevance in a first step. In the second step the user describes the task which has to be executed [20].

2.4 IsoMetrics

The survey corresponding to IsoMetrics consists of seven sub-scales with a total of 75 items. For each item the level of agreement and the subjective importance is scanned. Additionally participants can specify examples which relate to the item. IsoMetrics is mainly used for software evaluation from the user perspective and also follows the DIN EN ISO 9241-10 [18, 22–26].

2.5 Usability Testing of ERP Systems

The analysis of the mentioned measuring methods led to an "ERP usability test" with the dimensions emotion, software handling, efficiency, system support and learnability which were examined by 53 five point Likert scale items. These are derived from validated items of the existing surveys (Fig. 2).

existing surveys   ERP analysis range

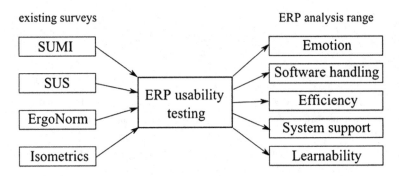

Fig. 2 Approach to ERP usability testing

3 Investigation

The "ERP usability test" was created and introduced in 2006. Meanwhile several surveys were conducted involving students and employees of companies gaining data and information regarding one or two distinct ERP systems or intra-company views on the running ERP system respectively ex-ante and ex-post evaluations during implementation projects [6]. The new survey was tested and validated with students at the University of Innsbruck who had to work with different ERP systems during their studies [6]. For the presented study the ERP usability test was used to evaluate the perceived usability from the perspective of users in companies working with an ERP system. The questions themselves are used without any adaptions except the change of the data collection method from a paper to an online survey. The survey is divided in two parts. Part A is capturing general data of an organisation. For example which ERP system is in use, how many users are working with it and how long the implementation phase lasted. As this data is consistent with all employees of one organisation, it had to be filled out only once per company. We contacted CIOs and other people in charge for the ERP system in organisations and invited them to fill out part A of the survey. They were furthermore asked to forward a link to part B of the survey together with a code to enable the link between data of all employees answering part B and the information the CIO entered in part A. Part B of the survey consisted of demographic data (12 items) and the ERP usability test itself. The five dimensions were queried by 7–13 items each with a total of 53 items. Each item asked for the level of agreement (from "strongly agree" to "don't agree at all") and the subjective importance (from "very important" to "not important at all") on a five point Likert scale. The survey was sent out to organisations in southern Germany and Austria by email in August 2014 to 42.222 recipients. A reminder was sent out early September 2014.

4   Results

Until November 2014 102 end users (part B) of 74 organisations (part A) participated in the survey. Involved organisations are located in Austria and Germany, are
active in various sectors and have a broad range of different ERP systems in use. On
average participating organisations have 206 employees. As usual in Austria and
southern Germany most of them are small enterprises as demonstrated in Fig. 3.

Concerning the amount of ERP users per organisation we can observe an
imbalance in favour of less users, as illustrated in Fig. 4. 60 % of the users classify
themselves as key users, the remaining 40 % as end users.

In a first step we calculated the mean evaluation of the five dimensions of the
ERP usability test depending on the amount of users working with the system in the
investigated organizations. The value 1 represents "strongly agree" whereas 5
stands for "don't agree at all". The values of negatively expressed items were
converted. Therefore any value in Fig. 5 below 3 indicates a positive evaluation of
the specific dimension of the usability. Higher values illustrate a more critical
evaluation by users, which can be observed in particular for the dimensions
learnability (LEA) and system support (SYS) on average. Participants who work in
organizations with 11 up to 50 ERP users show the best evaluation of all dimensions but LEA. The worst overall estimation of the usability can be observed by
participants who work in companies with 51–150 ERP users. As a trend we can
conclude, that participants of the two groups with less ERP users evaluate all five
dimensions of the usability higher than participants of the other groups.

In a second step we compared the results of the evaluation of the usability and
the subjective importance between the study conducted in 2006 [6] and the recent
data. In 2006 the respondents of the survey were students who had to work with
different ERP solutions for one semester during a lecture in contrast to users who
work with an ERP system at work. The results in Fig. 6 indicate that except for the
dimension system support (SYS) the evaluation of the usability is a lot more critical
by students in 2006.

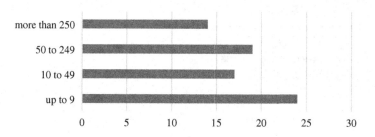

Fig. 3 Amount of employees

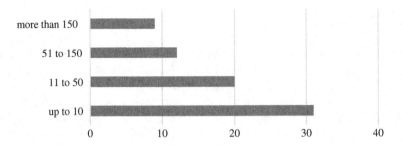

Fig. 4 Amount of ERP users

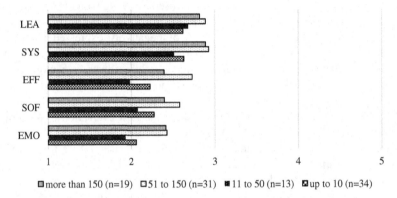

☐ more than 150 (n=19) ☐ 51 to 150 (n=31) ■ 11 to 50 (n=13) ☒ up to 10 (n=34)

Fig. 5 Evaluation of the usability dimensions by amount of users

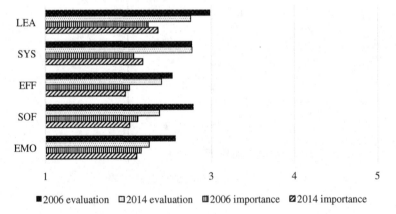

■ 2006 evaluation ☐ 2014 evaluation ⊞ 2006 importance ☒ 2014 importance

Fig. 6 Comparison of the results in 2006 and 2014

With respect to the number of participants the reason for this is not clear yet. There might be a general positive development of the usability of ERP systems within the last 8 years. But one can doubt that this is the only reason for the partly significant differences in perceived usability. The difference in the two samples concerning the length of experience with the system most likely affects the results, as well as the purpose of the use of the system. Students have to work with the ERP system to pass an exam whereas workers have to solve actual tasks in their own or at least their company's interest with support of the system.

Concerning the subjective importance we can observe that student respondents estimated the relevance of the items of the dimensions learnability (LEA) and system support (SYS) higher in comparison to the 2014 sample. The items of the dimensions efficiency (EFF), software handling (SOF) and emotion (EMO) are perceived slightly more important by participants in 2014.

In order to compare the evaluation of the overall usability for different ERP systems we centralized the data by subtracting the mean of each value for the usability and subjective importance. Figure 7 demonstrates the results, which are not representative due to the limited amount of participants so far.

The evaluated usability in Fig. 7 is presented on the horizontal axis, the subjective importance on the vertical one. The size of the bubbles represents the amount of participants who evaluated the specified group of ERP systems. Due to the number of participants we summarised data of participants who worked with the same group of systems as demonstrated in Table 2. We are aware that different versions within the same group may impose considerable differences in usability. In the interest of clarity however, some evaluated systems have been aggregated into

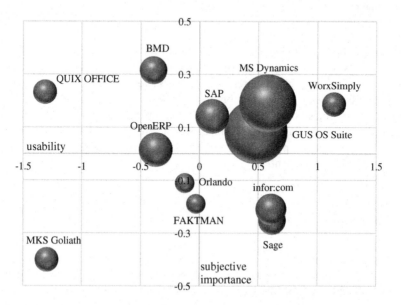

Fig. 7 Usability of different ERP system from the users' perspective [27]

Table 2 List of evaluated systems

Group	Version	Amount
GUS OS Suite	5.3	21
OpenERP	v7	5
	6.1	1
Orlando	Release 3.02 Build 461	1
	Build 442	1
Sage	Sage Classic Line 2015 4.5.0	2
	SAGE ERP b7 Rel. 6.1	2
SAP	SAP 6.0 EHP5	1
	SAP ECC 6.0 EPH5	1
	SAP 6	1
	SAP 3	1
	SAP ECC 6.0 700	1
	SAP R/3 ECC 6.0 EHP 0	1
WorxSimply	WorxSimply ERP 2014 v4.0.3.2	3
MS Dynamics	Microsoft Dynamics NAV 2009 R2	15
	Microsoft Navision 2013	2
infor:com	infor:com 7.1	5
BMD	BMD 5.5	2
	BMD 2014.17.02.96	1
	BMD NTSC 2014.17.02.113	1
FAKTMANN	V2.2	2
MKS Goliath	4.82B	3
QUIX OFFICE	5.305	3

one item labelled "group" in Table 2. The size of the bubbles indicates the amount of participants who evaluated the represented group of systems. As listed in detail in Table 2 the smallest bubbles represent two, the biggest one 21 evaluations. As we used centralized data, the centre of the axes represents the mean value of all evaluations. Bubbles positioned on the right side of the vertical axis therefore are evaluated with a usability above average. Bubbles below the horizontal axis indicate that surveyed users perceive the evaluation of the used items as less important than the average participant.

5 Conclusion

Due to the large number of system providers as well as various systems and releases in use a comparison of the perceived usability requires a huge amount of participants. The study demonstrates one approach to create and conduct a survey to measure the usability of ERP systems from the users' perspective and presents first results. Further data has to be collected to allow deeper analyses in upcoming research as well as to provide representativeness. Especially since ERP systems and their usability are relevant to the efficiency and effectiveness of end users' work this should be intensified.

References

1. Scott, J.E.: Technology acceptance and ERP documentation usability. Commun. ACM **51**(11), 121–124 (2008)
2. Somers, T., Nelson, K., Karimi, J.: Confirmatory factor analysis of the end-user computing satisfaction instrument: replication within an ERP domain. Decis. Sci. **34**(3), 595–621 (2003)
3. Nielsen, J., Coyne, K.P.: A useful investment: usability testing costs—but it pays for itself in the long run. CIO Mag. 15 Feb 2001
4. Juristo, N., Windl, H., Constantine, L.: Introducing usability. IEEE Softw. **18**(1), 20–21 (2001)
5. Paa, L., Ates, N.: Critical success factors of e-learning scenarios for ERP end-user training. In: Piazolo, F., Felderer, M. (eds.) Innovation and Future of Enterprise Information Systems, pp. 87–100. Springer, Berlin (2013)
6. Hinterhuber, H., Promberger, K., Piazolo, F.: Usability Testing von ERP-Systemen. Leopold-Franzens-Universität, Innsbruck (2006)
7. DIN, ENISO.: 9241-11 (1998) Ergonomische Anforderungen für Bürotätigkeiten mit Bildschirmgeräten–Teil 11: Anforderungen an die Gebrauchstauglichkeit; Leitsätze (ISO 9241-11: 1998). Beuth, Berlin
8. Geis, T., Hartwig, R.: Auf die Finger geschaut. Neue ISO-Norm für benutzergerechte interaktive Systeme. c't Magazin für Computertechnik **14**, 168–172 (1998)
9. Mutschler, B., Reichert, M.: Usability-Metriken als Nachweis der Wirtschaftlichkeit von Verbesserungen der Mensch-Maschine-Schnittstelle. In: Proceedings of the IWSM/MetriKon Workshop on Software Metrics (IWSM/MetriKon'04), Königs Wusterhausen, Germany, (2004)
10. Karat, C.: A business case approach to usability. In: Bias R., Mayhew, D. (eds.) Cost-Justifying Usability: An Update for an Internet Age, 2nd edn, Chapter 4, pp. 103–142 (2005)
11. Kirakowski, J.: The software usability measurement inventory: background and usage. In: Jordan, P., Thomas, B., Weedmeester, B. (eds.) Usability Evaluation in Industry, pp. 169–178. Taylor & Francis, London, (1996)
12. Macleod, M., Bowden, R., Bevan, N., Curson, I.: The MUSIC performance measurement method. Behav. Inf. Technol. **16**(4/5), 279–293 (1997)
13. Bevan, N., Curson, I.: Methods for Measuring Usability (1999)
14. Avouris, N.M.: An introduction to software usability. In: Proceedings of the 8th Panhellenic Conference on Informatics (Workshop on Software Usability), pp. 514–522 Nicosia, Athens (2001)
15. Macleod, M.: Usability in context: improving quality of use. In: Bradley, G., Hendricks, H.W. (eds.) Human Factors in Organizational Design and Management—IV (Proceedings of the International Ergonomics Association 4th International Symposium on Human Factors in Organizational Design and Management, Stockholm), Elsevier, Amsterdam, May 29–June 1 1994 (1994)
16. Kirakowski, J., Corbett, M.: SUMI: The software usability measurement inventory. Br. J. Educ. Technol. **24**(3), 210–212 (1993)

17. Laugwitz, B., Schrepp, M., Held, T.: Konstruktion eines Fragebogens zur Messung der User Experience von Softwareprodukten. SAP AG. In: Heinecke A.M., Paul, H. (Hrsg.): Mensch & Computer 2006: Mensch und Computer im Strukturwandel, pp. 125–134. Oldenbourg Verlag, München (2006)

18. Hamborg, K.-C., Gediga, G., Hassenzahl, M.: Fragebogen zur evaluation. In: Heinsen, S., Vogt, P. (Hrsg.): Usability praktisch umsetzen. Handbuch für Software, Web, Mobile Devices und andere innovative Produkte, pp. 171–186. Carl Hanser Verlag, München (2003)

19. Tullis, T., Albert, B.: Measuring the User Experience, Collecting, Analyzing and Presenting Usability Metrics. Morgen Kaufmann, Burlington (2008)

20. Dzida, W., Hofmann, B., Freitag, R., Redtenbacher, W., Baggen, R., Geis, T., Beimel, J., Zurheiden, C., Hampe-Neteler, W., Hartwig, R., Peters, H.: Gebrauchstauglichkeit von Software—ErgoNorm: Ein Verfahren zur Konformitätsprüfung von Software auf der Grundlage von DIN EN ISO 9241 Teile 10 und 11. Bundesanstalt für Arbeitsschutz und Arbeitsmedizin, Forschungsbericht (2000)

21. Schick, A.: Anforderungsanalyse für ein Feedbacksystem zur Verbesserung der Usability von Open-Source-Software. Diplomarbeit Fachbereich Informatik, Hamburg (2007)

22. Gediga, G., Hamborg, K.-C.: Heuristische evaluation und IsoMetrics: Ein Vergleich. In Liskowsky R., Velichkovsky, B.M., Wünschmann, W. (Hrsg.): Software-Ergonomie '97, Usability Engineering: Integration von Mensch-Computer-Interaktion und Software-Entwicklung, pp. 145–155. Stuttgart, Teubner (1997)

23. Gediga, G., Hamborg, K.-C.: IsoMetrics: an usability inventory supporting summative and formative evaluation of software systems. In: Bullinger, H.-J., Ziegler, J. (Hrsg.): Human-Computer Interaction, Ergonomics and User Interfaces, Proceedings of HCI International '99, vol. 1, pp. 1018–1022. Lawrence Erlbaum, Mahwah (1999)

24. Willumeit, H., Gediga, G., Hamborg, K.-C.: Validation of the IsoMetrics Usability Inventory. Forschungsberichte Nr. 105, Fachbereich Psychologie, Universität Osnabrück (1995)

25. Hamborg, K.-C.: Gestaltungsunterstützende evaluation von Software: Zur Effektivität und Effizienz des IsoMetrics (L) Verfahrens. In: Herczeg, M., Prinz, W., Oberquelle, H. (Hrsg.): Mensch und Computer 2002: Vom interaktiven Werkzeug zu kooperativen Arbeits- und Lernwelten, pp. 303–312. Stuttgart, B.G., Teubner (2002)

26. Christophersen, T.: Usability im online-shopping. Entwicklung eines Fragebogeninstrumentes (ufosV2) unter Berücksichtigung formativer und reflektiver Messmodelle. Dissertation, Christian-Albrechts-Universität Kiel (2006)

27. Paa, L., Promberger, K., Keckeis, J.: Messung der ERP-Usability. ERP Manag. **4**, 29–31 (2014)c

Part V
Business Intelligence Strategy

Impacts of SAP HANA on Business Intelligence (BI) Strategy Formulation

Eva-Maria Furtner, Harald Wildhölzl, Norbert Schlager-Weidinger
and Kurt Promberger

Abstract Many organizations are still focusing their BI activities solely on reporting (descriptive analytics). Since reports inherently provide information that just results in reactive measures rather than proactive and innovative actions, the outcome frequently implicate competitive disadvantage through slower discovery of insights, slower reaction times, and decreased abilities to effectively steer the company. Hence, the usage of BI technologies in companies should be expanded up to a point where business users are able to understand "Why" a business event is happening, instead of just receiving an answer on "What" has happened [1, 2]. With an effective and efficient BI environment, organizations are able to increase the value of the business sustainably [3].

1 Introduction and Background

Many companies cannot rely on their reporting and planning systems because they contain multiple sources of truth. Business analysts are often gathering and processing data instead of analysing data because of data quality problems or unclear business logic. Reasons include the organic growth of a company, BI strategy that is not aligned with corporate strategy or too little investment in BI toolsets. In order to realize the objective of a single point of truth, a transparent business logic, a

E.-M. Furtner (✉) · H. Wildhölzl · N. Schlager-Weidinger
IVM Institut für Verwaltungsmanagement GmbH, Innsbruck, Austria
e-mail: eva.furtner@verwaltungsmanagement.at

H. Wildhölzl
e-mail: harald.wildhoelzl@verwaltungsmanagement.at

N. Schlager-Weidinger
e-mail: norbert.schlager-weidinger@verwaltungsmanagement.at

K. Promberger
University of Innsbruck, Innsbruck, Austria
e-mail: kurt.promberger@uibk.ac.at

© Springer International Publishing Switzerland 2016   163
F. Piazolo and M. Felderer (eds.), *Multidimensional Views on Enterprise
Information Systems*, Lecture Notes in Information Systems and Organisation 12,
DOI 10.1007/978-3-319-27043-2_13

strategically aligned management control process and a BI roadmap has to be set up. These points take into consideration the three dimensions of people, processes and technology.

2 Business Intelligence

If businesses are able to reach this level of maturity in their BI environment, they are able to get to the root of the trouble when problems occur or when the business environment and external requirements change. Consequently, in order to create value for a business, a BI environment has to achieve a level of excellence where the different aspects and parts of a company are aligned and run smoothly. The term "BI Excellence" describes the combined and comprehensive elaboration of strategy, people, processes, and technologies with the overall goal of creating impact, value, and effectiveness in the business [4]. A comprehensive approach of strategy (e.g. development of a strategy map and balanced scorecard), people (e.g. agreement and strong involvement of senior management and implementation of BI competence center), processes (e.g. development of a KPI framework to monitor and adjust processes) and technologies (e.g. implementation of an enterprise data warehouse that guarantees a single point of truth to support people and processes) is needed in order to achieve BI excellence [5]. This implies that a BI strategy can only be successful if it includes all three dimensions, the people, the processes, and the technology. Issues and tasks that arise within the BI environment always have to be addressed by all three dimensions, as illustrated in the cube below. This holistic approach guarantees that end-users will experience significant increases in satisfaction, which also increases the acceptance of the BI environment. Subsequently, the BI maturity level of the company will be increased (Fig. 1).

Fig. 1 Holistic approach of BI strategy

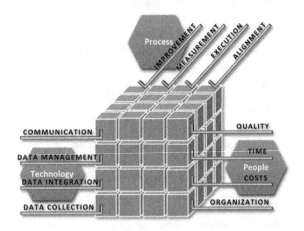

3   In-Memory Computing Powered by SAP HANA (High Performance Analytic Appliance)

SAP HANA is an in-memory data platform that is deployable as an on premise appliance, or in the cloud. It is a platform, which is best suited for performing real-time analytics, and developing and deploying real-time applications.

3.1   In-Memory Computing

In-memory computing in general is emerging into an applied field that every organization should take into consideration when making decisions influencing the future landscape of its BI and Business Process Management (BPM) environment. From a technological standpoint, in-memory computing has been available for decades as the technical foundations were laid in the 1980s [6]. However, positive developments in the hardware industry in the last few years have made the application of in-memory technologies economically viable. Those developments include increased main memory (RAM) and lower cost computing power [7]. This explains why in-memory computing, despite the existence of parallel computing since the mid-1980s, was not a relevant approach for data storage and analysis until recently [8]. Today, whole enterprise database systems can be permanently moved to main memory systems, which are called in-memory database management systems (IMDBMS) [9]. There are five main characteristics of in-memory computing:

- First, instead of storing data on hard drives like relational database management systems (RDBMS), the data is loaded in its entirety and stored in the internal main memory of the computer. Since main memory can be directly accessed by the CPUs, access times are significantly faster [10]. To maximize CPU performance it is necessary to minimize the bottleneck between main memory and the CPU cache. Cache load can be reduced by using consecutive and sequential data sets to harness a column-oriented approach, which is also beneficial for OLAP [11].
- Second, within an IMDBMS both, row- and column-oriented storage can be used, whereas RDBMS just use row-oriented data storage. Row oriented storage provides significant advantages when single tuples are read. The column-storage approach is advantageous when calculations or aggregates are performed on just a few columns [12].
- Third, in-memory technology uses multi-core CPUs that enable parallel data processing, increasing the processing of operations and performance exponentially [13]. A multitude of operations can be performed simultaneously when algorithms and queries are divided across several processing units [14].
- Fourth, column-oriented storage enables compression procedures that considerably reduces data size. Despite fast growing main memory capacities, it is still

necessary to use data compression techniques to minimize the amount of data. An experiment by Plattner and Zeier illustrated that it is possible to reduce one terabyte of customer data on a hard-disk to 100 GB of in-memory storage by efficiently using compression [12].

• Fifth, IMDBMS exclusively use an insert-only method, meaning that update or delete actions are not possible. Changes to existing data in the database is limited to illustrating whether data is valid or invalid based on flags or time stamps. This method allows the system to track changes and keep a history. This is often legally required by many countries and it provides more insights for companies due to better record keeping of company actions over time [15].

3.2 SAP HANA

SAP HANA consists of real-time analytics and real-time applications. With real-time analytics real-time operational reporting of transaction data is possible. In Data Warehousing (SAP BW on HANA) the performance is boosted. Queries should run 10–100 times faster, data loads 5–10 times faster and calculations 5–10 times faster. SAP HANA offers a platform, which can be used for a variety of applications, not only SAP. Furthermore, it is possible to leverage text analysis on Big Data.

These real-time analytics are enabled by real-time applications as core process accelerators, for planning and optimization as well for sense and response apps. The core process accelerators replicate transactional data into HANA in order to take advantage of in-memory-computing. The planning optimization app is an application which pushes complex requests to the data base and allows a fast computation for the required results. The sense and response app offers a text search and mining as well as predictive analytics for data-intensive processes. Earlier performance constraints can be solved by SAP HANA [16].

4   Case Study

In a cooperation with an Austrian manufacturing & engineering company the University of Innsbruck conducted a case study in order to assess the impact of SAP HANA on BI strategy formulation and execution. Therefore, a data set was exported from the company's SAP ERP system (COPA = Controlling & Profitability Analysis Module) and stored in flat files (.csv). Just the fact table consisted of more than six million rows, over two hundred columns, and more than six gigabytes of data.

The main focus of the study was the utilization of SAP HANA to compute a contribution margin calculation. The fact and dimension tables were loaded into the

SAP HANA environment in order to create a functional prototype to demonstrate whether or not SAP HANA has an impact on the setup and modelling of a BI project, on the acceptance rate of BI within a company, and its influence on planning activities. The prototype was implemented in a cloud environment hosted by Amazon Web Services. The SAP environment consisted of the following: a fully operational SAP HANA appliance, the data management and modelling tool SAP Business Warehouse, various data presentation tools from SAP Business Objects like Design Studio to create dashboards, Web Intelligence to build flexible intuitive ad hoc reports, Crystal Reports to generate pixel-precise standard reports, and finally Predictive Analysis software, a planning and forecasting tool. The case study aimed to answer the following research questions:

RQ1 Does SAP HANA change the setup of a BI project?
RQ2 Does SAP HANA increase the acceptance rate of BI during the implementation process and when operating?
RQ3 How does SAP HANA effect the modelling of BI projects? Does SAP HANA increase the cycle time of a BI implementation project?
RQ4 How does SAP HANA affect the architecture of a classical EDWH?

4.1   Setup of a BI Project with SAP HANA (RQ1)

The data set of the company's ERP system (COPA) was loaded directly into SAP HANA without using SAP Business Warehouse (SAP BW) data objects. The aim was to simulate rapid prototyping in an early stage of the BI project, to gather information about the data quality and semantic coherences. As a result the extent of necessary business transformations could be derived and a dialogue with business departments could be accomplished on a practical basis in consideration of the real database. The involvement of the stakeholder could be assured. Despite the practical approach, all three dimensions process, people and technology still needed to be addressed. On closer inspection of the three dimensions different challenges were identified. Regarding the process dimension the challenge of not drawing attention to definitions is even higher due to the practical approach. Results can be achieved very quickly and the focus on long-term architecture can easily move to the background. Nonetheless in order to reach standardization and a single point of truth, organizational as well as technical definitions are necessary. For example with the people dimension, the inclusion of BI stakeholders in an early stage improves communication processes, but these processes have to be emphasized actively in order to avoid challenges in later stages of the project. Taking a closer look at the technology dimension, it can be deduced that the establishment of an EDWH-approach is still needed and specific features of DWH environments have to be taken into account. Definitions regarding business transformations and DWH-architecture have to be precisely determined. Another challenge, especially when considering SAP BW on HANA, is the toolset orchestration. In particular, the interaction of SAP BW and SAP HANA toolsets has to be taken into account in order to find the right technological approach and toolset for each requirement ranging from highly-conformed key figure models to flexible near-time BI. The toolset options range from Netweaver based BEx (Business Explorer), the SAP Business Objects toolset to SAP Lumira, SAP Fiori components and so on.

4.2   Acceptance Rate in Implementation Process (RQ2)

The study showed that with SAP HANA rapid prototyping is possible as immediate value could be derived from the loaded data and provided to BI stakeholders. These stakeholders were able to confirm the validity of reports so that information quality could be verified at an early stage. Misunderstandings were avoided as the data quality was assured very early. The acceptance rate of SAP HANA rose considerably when the reports were presented. The complexity could be hidden as calculations moved to the database layer and queries which could not be executed earlier due to performance restrictions could be executed with SAP HANA. The data management and integration was very flexible, which is favourable on the one hand, but on the other hand it has to be controlled closely as not everybody should have the opportunity to manage data in their own way in order to guarantee a single source of truth. As direct access to data is possible (without the introduction of further layers) complexity diminishes. Only the interchange of the tools leads to higher complexity as the user has to define the demanded toolset in advance.

4.3   Modelling of BI Projects (RQ3)

The early integration of stakeholders mentioned previously as well as the assurance of data quality from the beginning allowed very fast reaction to data quality problems. Reports can be built in early stages of a project. Therefore, it was necessary to define a virtualization layer to determine a single time that did not change throughout the project. It was very important for the manufacturing & engineering company to have a single point of truth in reporting and management control across the company. In order to fulfil this requirement, additional layers had to be added as the following figure shows.

Figure 2 can be interpreted as a process model for reaching a single point of truth in a company. The data can be confirmed and reviewed in an early stage by just loading data in SAP HANA tables and views (as seen on the left side of the figure). By adding step-by-step supplementary data layers, the conformity of data rises and a single point of view can be achieved by definition and usage of conformed dimensions as well as predefined business transformations and unified definitions of

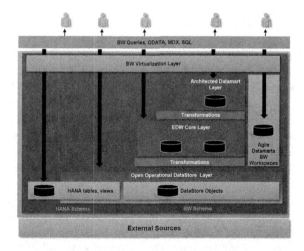

Fig. 2 Layered scalable architecture LSA++-concept [17]

key performance indicators. In the implementation process agile process models can be used. This leads to a reduced cycle time in the BI implementation project due to assessments and assurance of data quality and definitions.

4.4 Architecture of BI Project (RQ4)

BI projects should not only be considered as reporting activities, planning and forecasting has to be taken into account. SAP HANA offers a combined use of data for reporting and planning and thereby supports the management controlling process. In SAP HANA, new virtual modelling objects like Analytic Views, Calculation Views, Composite Provider, Open ODS Views and Transient Provider are introduced. The SAP BW objects, which are physical modelling objects, remain. This leads to the consideration of when to use virtual versus physical layers. In order to reach conformity of data and a single point of truth, it is necessary to pursue the LSA++ concept as well as an Enterprise Data Warehouse approach.

In the past years, the front-end-tools of SAP have been further developed. With regards to reporting and planning this means that DesignStudio and Analysis for Office can now be used for reporting and planning. This results in a necessity to define tools used within the company. In conclusion it can be said that clear definition is needed in order to leverage the offered objects and tools optimally for the company.

5   Conclusion

The strategic focus of SAP is put on SAP HANA, not only as the database but also as a platform for all further development. It is a change in architecture like R/2 to R/3 was. The case study showed that the (Enterprise) Data Warehouse approach is still needed. SAP HANA offers a greater flexibility, which has to be populated by company guidelines. The new SAP HANA objects have to be subsumed into an architectural construct. Therefore, guidelines are essential, which consider the interplay between virtual and physical data management. In projects with SAP HANA, improvements in development cycle times can be identified, leading to a higher acceptance of stakeholders through early adoption. Data quality issues can be recognized early. In order to leverage these opportunities, a change in project management is essential. Project management will change from waterfall process models to an agile form of project management, like rapid prototyping. It can be concluded that organizational requirements still exist, leading the necessity of a top-down modelling (defining key figures and conformed dimensions overall in a first step), as well as a single point of modelling.

References

1. Galberaith, S.: Midmarket insights: 'Why' reporting alone isn't a strong enough business intelligence strategy. http://www.gartner.com/technol-ogy/reprints.do?id=1-1I4BR0R&ct=130805&st=sg (2013)
2. Davenport, T.H.: What do we talk when we talk about analytics? In: Davenport, T.H. (ed.) Enterprise analytics, optimize performance, process and decision through big data, pp. 9–18. Pearson Education, Upper Saddle River (2013)
3. Olszak, C.M., Ziemba, E.: Critical success factors for implementing business intelligence systems in small and medium enterprises on the example of upper Silesia, Poland. Interdisc. J. Inf. Knowl. Manage. **7**, 129–151 (2012)
4. Boyer, J.: Business Intelligence Strategy: A Practical Guide for Achieving BI Excellence. MC Press, Ketchum (2010)
5. Hawking, P.: Business intelligence excellence: a company's journey to business intelligence maturity. Int. J. Technol. Knowl. Soc. **8**(2), 91–99 (2012)
6. Eich, M.H.: Database machines and knowledge base machines. Kluwer Int. Ser. Eng. Comput. Sci. **43**, 325–338 (1988)
7. Vom Brocke, J., Debortoli, S., Müller, O., Reuter, N.: How in-memory technology can create business value: insights from The Hilti Case. Commun. Assoc. Inf. Syst. **34**, 151–168 (2014)
8. Bain, W.: Using in-memory computing to simplify big data analytics. http://www.datanami.com/datanami/2012-10-02/using_in-memory_computing_to_simplify_big_data_analytics.html (2012)
9. Wust, J., Boese, J.-H., Renkes, F., Blessing, S., Krueger, J., Plattner, H.: Efficient logging for enterprise workloads on column-oriented in-memory databases. In: Chen, X., Lebanon, G., Wang, H., Zaki, M.J. (eds.) Proceedings of the 21st ACM International Conference on Information and Knowledge Management, pp. 2085–2089. ACM, Maui, Hawaii (2012)
10. Knabke, T., Olbrich, S.: Towards agile BI: applying in-memory technology to data warehouse architectures. In: Lehner, W., Piller, G. (eds.) Proceedings zur Tagung Innovative Unternehmensanwendungen mit In-Memory Data Management, pp. 101–114 (2011)

11. Sharma, S.: Big data landscape. Int. J. Sci. Res. Publ. **3**(6), 861–868 (2013)
12. Plattner, H., Zeier, A.: In-Memory Data Management: An Inflection Point for Enterprise Applications. Springer, Berlin (2011)
13. Word, J.: SAP HANA Essential, 3rd edn. Epistemy Press, Frisco (2013)
14. Chaudhuri, S., Dayal, U., Narasayya, V.: An overview of business intelligence technology. Commun. ACM **54**(8), 88–98 (2011)
15. Grund, M., Krueger, J., Tinnefeld, C., Zeier, A.: Vertical partitioning in insert-only scenarios for enterprise applications. In: Qi, E. (ed.), 16th International Conference on Industrial Engineering and Engineering Management, pp. 760–765. IEEE, Beijing, China (2009)
16. http://www.saphana.com/docs/DOC-2272. Accessed Jan 2015
17. Haupt, J.: LSA++ (Layered Scalable Architecture) for SAP NetWeaver on SAP HANA. EIM 203. SAP AG. http://www.sdn.sap.com/irj/scn/go/portal/prtroot/docs/library/uuid/7076b1f6-e942-3010-d1b9-ecd1416458a5?QuickLink=index&overridelayout=true&57909044127356 (2012)

Part VI
Public Sector

Sequence of Contracts as a Means of Planning in ERP-Systems

Bjoern Kemmoona

Abstract In local government planning, nether the single department nor politicians do exactly know, which financial planning data they can really decide on and what decision will bring which (direct and indirect) financial and legal aftermath. Governmental tasks and subsequently actions as well as resources are widely predetermined by legal, technical and commercial norms—especially in local authorities. The actions resp. the therefore needed resources are provided by contracts. From these contracts, finanical planning data can be derived. The presented concept of "contract based planning" shows, how these connections can be used for governmental planning and how ERP-Systems can support this logic.

Keywords Contracts · Public sector · Planning support · Enterprise resource planning

1 Introduction

The research attempt of this paper is to outline a new methodology (supported by ERP-systems) of financial planning in local authorities, using the knowledge of juristical connections between the elements of planning. It will be shown, that by the usage of legal, technical and commercial norms—combined with the information that can be derived from contracts connected to the elements of planning— a local authority can get knowledge of (a) which actions and resources to be used and (b) what the (direct and indirect) financial effects of those actions and resources are.

To develop this methodology, the juristical environment and its appearance within the planning process of local authorities is presented (Chap. 2). Based on this environment, the paper shows the basic conceptual elements of the planning

B. Kemmoona (✉)
Business Information Systems, University of Paderborn, Paderborn, Germany
e-mail: bjoern.kemmoona@wiwi.upb.de
URL: http://winfo1-www.upb.de

© Springer International Publishing Switzerland 2016   175
F. Piazolo and M. Felderer (eds.), *Multidimensional Views on Enterprise Information Systems*, Lecture Notes in Information Systems and Organisation 12,
DOI 10.1007/978-3-319-27043-2_14

methodology (Chap. 3) and outlines the architecture of an ERP-implementation (Chap. 4). At the end, a short conclusion with a set of further research question will be given (Chap. 5).

2 Planning in Local Authorities—An Environment of Legal Restrictions

The tasks of local authorities[1] are differentiated as follows [3, pp. 246 ff., 20, pp. 35 ff.]:

- imperative compulsory tasks:[2] no decision whether "*if*" or "*how*" the task has to be done (for example elections, population census, etc.)
- compulsory tasks: no decision about "*if*" it has to be done, but free to decide "*how*" (for example offering schools, clarification plants, etc. but also compulsory risk prevention like flood prevention, local disaster control, etc.)
- voluntary tasks: free to decide "*if*" and "*how*" it has to be done (for example theaters, awarding club grants, etc.).

These tasks are restricted by legal (e.g. local, regional and federal law), technical (e.g. DIN standards [8]) and commercial norms (e.g. "Construction Contract Procedures"—VOB [6]). These norms define which actions are to be taken[3] and which resources to use (in terms of quality and/or quantity).[4]

Without regarding any targets, the yearly governmental planning is already limited by these restrictions. A special restriction is the requirement of a balanced budget (on a longterm-view within the planning-periods—refer to [5, 17, 18] for more detail) at the end of the planning process. The finance department and the local politicians define the financial high-level parameters at the beginning of the planning process [20, p. 276]. Afterwards, the other departments (e.g. school administration department) start their (decentralised) planning that results in a document containing financial values for each product (-group) provided by the department—aggregated by payment category.[2, p. 96, 21, pp. 113 ff.] This document is then to be discussed and approved by political boards (Fig. 1).

In some forms of local government management, [18] the planning document additionaly provides targets as an agreement between the department and politics.[5] The (mostly abstract) targets (e.g. "introducing new media in secondary schools") can be reached by different actions (e.g. "introducing digital whiteboards in all

---

[1]We are going to take the local authorities in Germany—especially NRW—as an example.

[2]These orders come from either the regional government authority or the federal administration—sometimes turning European law into local tasks.

[3]See Sect. 3 for a more sophisticated view.

[4]The restrictions coming from contracts are added in Sect. 3.

[5]The reason is to let the politics decide about the "*what*" and the department about the "*how*".

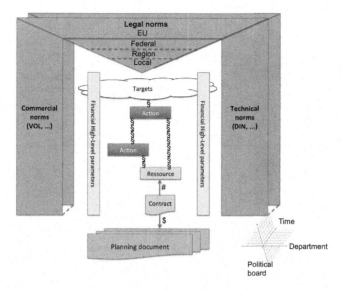

Fig. 1 Restrictions on local governmental planning [4]

rooms", "installing media-corners in every main classrooms", etc.). All these actions (whether they are explicitly named in the planning document or not) bring different (direct or indirect) aftermath by other actions and/or resources required by legal, technical or commercial norms. It might also be, that the aftermath conflicts with other restrictions brought by compulsory/voluntary tasks or derived from other targets of the same/another department to be discussed and approved by the same/another political board. Figure 2 presents an example of possible aftermath for the "introduction of new media in secondary schools".

The priorisation and weighting of these (sometimes competing [13]) targets is one of the main parts of the discussion within the political boards (especially in the "main and financial committees" and the city council). As a prerequisite, the department as well as the politicians need to know their scope of planning in terms of:

1. What elements of the financial planning are predetermined?

   (a) What are predetermined (direct and indirect) actions and resources (due to the type of task and/or legal, technical and commercial norms)?
   (b) What financial values derive from these actions and resources?

2. What are the financial and legal effects of implementing political targets?

   (a) What are possible and predefined (direct or indirect) actions and resources?
   (b) Which financial values derive from these actions and resources?
   (c) Do they juristically conflict with other predefined or planned actions and resources?

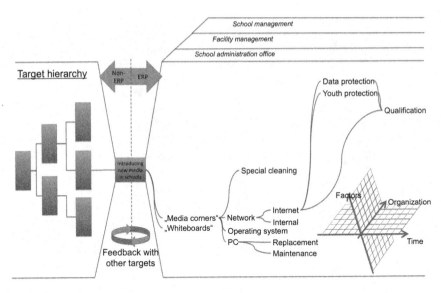

Fig. 2 Part of targets aftermath (example)

In the following section, we outline the basic principles of "contract based planning" to introduce a planning-methodology that can help to give an answer to these questions.

3   Contract Based Planning as a Means of Transparency

The above mentioned governmental tasks and/or targets can have varying legal consequences which are in a sophisticated status, depending on time and/or other conditions:

- an *obligation* can exist (e.g. inclusion of handicapped kids in schools, but not before 2014) or be active (e.g. obligation of special cleaning of media corners in schools, due to the technical norm DIN 77400 [9]). An obligation can be followed or violated (without legal consequence if not active).
- a *prohibition* can exist (e.g. the prohibition of putting photos of kids on the schools website) or be active (e.g. the prohibition of putting photos of kids on the schools website without permission of the parents). A prohibition can also be followed or violated (without legal consequence if not active).
- a *right* can exist (e.g. inclusion of handicapped kids in schools) or be exercisable (e.g. inclusion of handicapped kids in schools after the beginning of 2014). A right can also be exercised or become extinct. As a right is "everything that is not prohibited" [14], not all imaginable rights are relevant for governmental planning. We restrict the analysis to those rights, that are explicitly mentioned in

legal, technical or commercial norms or that have been successfully proved by other organizations, especially other local authorities.

These legal consequences determine sequences of actions and resources such as: "When you are implementing media corners in schools (action), there is an existent obligation of building them accessable to disabled persons which is active since 2014. The action also results in the obligation of special fire protection (active by the action of implementing media corners) which implies the obligation of periodical inspections (active by the action of special fire protection). These inspections need to be done by resources with a defined qualification and quantity (also active obligation)".

Resources (like the qualified resources of the above example) are normally provided through contracts (e.g. employment contract, framework contract). They define the resources (goods and services) provided (in time, quantity and quality) as well as the subsequent future payments (time and amount) [11, p. 10, 19, pp. 409 ff.]. So contracts can operate as a link between actions, respectively their required resources and the financial planning values. Contracts themselves can lead to legal consequences by their own clauses (e.g. need of external inspection in the buying contract of digital whiteboards) or by subsequent legal aftermath because of legal, technical or commercial norms. These consequences might again lead to actions and/or resources that will be provided by other contracts or might conflict with legal consequences of other contracts and/or norms. The result is a tree of actions and resources with legal consequences as branches and contracts as leaves (Fig. 3).

The local authority is bound by these contracts at least for a certain time, [11, p. 10] specified within the contract (e.g. cleaning services) or a subsequent legal norm (e.g. employment contract). So the financial values within this timeframe are fixed (e.g. salary in the next period of notice—which can be a long time for public officals). These contracts and the resources they provide can only be utilized for

Fig. 3 Tree of actions, resources and contracts (extract)

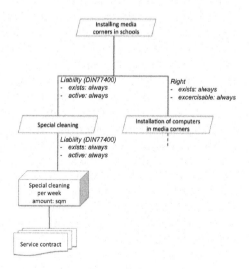

other (similar/dissimilar) tasks, but they cannot be exchanged by other contracts. After the next period of notice, the contract (and the subsequent financial payments) can be withdrawn. But there is a necessity of a new contractual agreement as far as the underlying legal requirement is still active. Contracts can only be withdrawn without substitute if there is no (direct or indirect) legal consequence, demanding the provided resources. The legal consequences can change over time, as well as the organizational and political responsibility for the affected actions, resources and contracts.

So the process of planning is no more a process of financial forecast by the department, but a process of planning actions, resources and contracts according to legal restrictions. The amount and complexity of legal, technical and commercial norms as well as the legal consequences of the contracts within a local government is too large and widespread to be handled by a department on its own. ERP-Systems that are already the technical instrument for governmental planning can help by providing a logic according to the concept of contract based planning.

4 Implementing Contract Based Planning into ERP-Systems

Two elements are essential for implementing the logic of contract based planning into ERP-Systems:

- a *reference model* that contains all the above mentioned elements and their connections
- a central *business object "contract"* that provides information about provided resources, derived financial values and periods of notice

The reference model [24, S.5, 10, S. 131, 22, S. 66, 69–74, 1, S. 90, 25, S. 31–38] contains legal, technical and commercial norms as well as affected reference elements of (abstract formulated) targets, actions, resources and contract types. It also incloses the above mentioned connections between these elements. Targets, actions, resources and contracts can be "instantiated", i.e. connected with an existing element within the ERP-System and connected to legal restrictions (Fig. 4).

At the end of the instantiation, the ERP-System can verify e.g. whether all neccesary resources (defined by norms relevant for the defined tasks and targets) are provided by an existing contract, if there are more contracts needed or if there are contracts providing resources not needed for the planned actions. It can also check, if there are any juristical conflicts within the aftermath of chosen and/or derived actions. After the instantiation is completed, financial planning data can be derived from the contracts and be transferred into the planning structure [11].

To do this efficiently, a central business object "contract" is needed, which has to be at least able to represent which resources it provides (time, quality and quantity) and what financial data it generates. The result is financial planning data of three

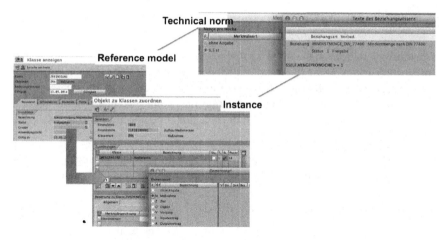

Fig. 4 Instantiating an action with a legal restriction (example)

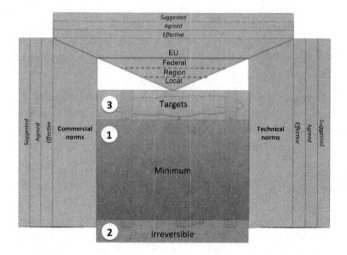

Fig. 5 Categories of derived financial planning data

categories (Fig. 5). The first one is the financial minimum, based on what the government has to do due to legal, technical and commercial norms (derived by the providing contracts). The second one is that minimum plus the irreversible financial data due to contracts in general (no matter if they are used or not). The third one is the minimum plus irreversible plus the additional legal consequences (not already existent in the minimum) due to voluntary targets/actions.

5   Conclusion and Requirements

With the implementation of contract based planning in ERP-Systems, it is possible to provide information to the local authority about which part of the financial planning is predetermined and what the (financial and legal) effects of political targets are. This demands technically the implementation of a central contract-object and the integration of a reference model. The organizational perspective also seems to be challenging as

1. the initial process of instantiating the reference model and its updates is laborious and it requires the will to make the reasons for financial planning data transparent
2. the reference model has to be built, delivered and updated.

The first challenge depends on the will for transparency by the local government. The second challenge can be an opportunity for the suppliers of ERP-Systems that can

- establish a standard format for exchanging legal, technical and commercial norms and the elements of the reference model [4, 7, 12, 15, 16, 23].
- bring together possible publishers of knowledge relevant to the reference model (local authorities, their unions as well as providers of legal, technical and commercial norms).

More research needs to be done if this logic can also be transferred to the industrial sector, especially in international scenarios where different (country-specific) types of connections between the elements of the reference model can exist.

References

1. Becker, J., Holten, R., Knackstedt, R., Schuette, R.: Referenz-Informationsmodellierung. In: Bodendorf, F., Grauer, M. (eds.) Verbundtagung Wirtschaftsinformatik (2000)
2. Bernhardt, H., Mutschler, K., Stockel-Veltmann, C.: Kommunales Finanzmanagement NRW, vol. 6. Verlag Bernhardt-Witten (2010)
3. Bogumil, J.: Kommunale Aufgabenwahrnehmung im Wandel: Kommunalisierung, Regionalisierung und Territorialreform in Deutschland und Europa (Stadtforschung Aktuell). VS Verlag fuer Sozialwissenschaften (2010)
4. Brandt, C.: Vom Vertragsmanagement zur zwischenbetrieblichen Kommunikation. Innovation Publication (2009)
5. Bundesministeriums der Justiz und fuer Verbraucherschutz: Gesetz zur Foerderung der Stabilitaet und des Wachstums der Wirtschaft. Bundesdruckerei (2006)
6. Bundesministerium fuer Verkehr, Bau und Stadtentwicklung: Vergabe- und Vertragsordnung fuer Bauleistungen—VOB. Bundesdruckerei (2012)
7. Daskalopulu, A., Maibaum, T.: Towards electronic contract performance. In: 12th International Workshop on Database and Expert Systems Applications. IEEE (2001)
8. Deutsches Institut fuer Normung e. V.: http://www.din.de/ (2014)

9. DIN Deutsches Institut fuer Normung e.V: DIN 77400:2003-09, Deutsche Norm—Reinigungsdienstleistungen Schulgebaeude Anforderungen an die Reinigung. Beuth Verlag (2003)
10. Fischer, J.: Informationswirtschaft: Anwendungssysteme. Oldenbourg Verlag (1999)
11. Fischer, J.: Vertragsmanagement in Wertschoepfungsnetzen. Skizze eines Forschungsprogramms aus Sicht eines Wirtschaftsinformatikers. In: Blecker, Th., Gemuenden, J. (eds.) Wertschoepfungsnetzwerke Festschrift fuer Prof. Dr. Bernd Kaluza (2006)
12. Grosof B.N., Labrou, Y., Chan, H.Y.: A declarative approach to business rules in contracts: courteous logic programs in XML. In: Proceedings of the 1st ACM Conference on Electronic Commerce. ACM (1999)
13. Heinen, E.: Grundlagen betriebswirtschaftlicher Entscheidungen. Das Zielsystem der Unternehmung, vol. 3. Gabler Verlag (1976)
14. Herberger, M., Simon, D.: Wissenschaftstheorie fuer Juristen. Alfred Metzner Verlag (1980)
15. Kabilan, V., Johannesson, P.: Semantic Representation of Contract Knowledge using Multi Tier Ontology (2003)
16. Karlapalem, K., Dani, A.R., Krishna, R.R.: A frame work for modeling electronic contracts. In: Conceptual Modeling—ER 2001—20th International Conference on Conceptual Modeling. Springer (2001)
17. Keynes, J.M.: Allgemeine Theorie der Beschaeftigung, des Zinses und des Geldes, vol. 9. Duncker & Humblot (2002)
18. Ministerium fuer Inneres und Kommunales des Landes Nordrhein-Westfalen: Neues Kommunales Finanzmanagement in Nordrhein-Westfalen. Bundesdruckerei (2010)
19. Riebel, P.: Einzelkosten- und Deckungsbeitragsrechnung: Grundfragen einer markt- und entscheidungsorientierten Unternehmensrechnung, vol. 14. Gabler Verlag (1994)
20. Schwarting, G.: Der kommunale Haushalt: Haushaltswirtschaft—Haushaltssteuerung—Kameralistik und Doppik. Erich Schmidt Verlag (2006)
21. Schwarting, G.: Effizienz in der Kommunalverwaltung—Dezentrale Verantwortung, Produkte, Budgets und Controlling. Erich Schmidt Verlag (2005)
22. Schuette, R.: Grundsaetze Ordnungsmaessiger Referenzmodellierung: Konstruktion konfigurations- und anpassungsorientierter Modelle. Gabler Verlag (1997)
23. Tan, Y.-H., Thoen, W.: Using event semantics for modeling contracts. In: Proceedings of the 35th Hawaii International Conference on System Sciences (2002)
24. Thomas, O.: Das Referenzmodellverstaendnis in der Wirtschaftsinformatik: Historie, Literaturanalyse und Begriffsexplikation. In: IWi—Veroeffentlichungen des Instituts fuer Wirtschaftsinformatik im Deutschen Forschungszentrum fuer Kuenstliche Intelligenz, vol. 187. (2006)
25. Vom Brocke, J.: Referenzmodellierung : Gestaltung und Verteilung von Konstruktionsprozessen. Adv. Inf. Syst. Manag. Sci. **4**, (2003)